PARTING WITH A CHILD
FOR ADOPTION:
THE MOTHERS' PERSPECTIVE

PUBLISHED BY
BRITISH AGENCIES FOR
ADOPTION & FOSTERING
11 SOUTHWARK STREET
LONDON SE1 1RQ
© BAAF 1991
ISBN 0 903534 99 1
DESIGNED BY ANDREW HAIG
TYPESET BY SET TWO CREATIVE TYPESETTING
PRINTED AND BOUND IN ENGLAND

Photographs posed by models.
Front cover: John Birdsall Photography;
back cover: Michelle Williams.

DISCUSSION SERIES : 14

Parting with a child for adoption

the mother's perspective

◆

*Patricia Bouchier, Lydia Lambert
and John Triseliotis*

BRITISH AGENCIES FOR
ADOPTION & FOSTERING

About the authors

Patricia Bouchier has been a child care practitioner in both statutory and voluntary agencies in Scotland for the past 17 years. She is a member of the Panel of Curators and Reporting Officers for Lothian Region, the current Chair of the National Association for the Welfare of Children in Hospital (Scotland) and of the Friends of SARA (Scottish AIDS Research Appeal). The research into the experiences of relinquishing mothers was undertaken during a post-graduate attachment to the University of Edinburgh.

Lydia Lambert, Research Fellow at Edinburgh University, was a diocesan social worker before becoming a researcher at ABAA (now BAAF) and then the National Children's Bureau. Previous publications include: *Children who wait* (with Jane Rowe, ABAA, 1973); *Children in changing families* (Macmillan, 1980); *Achieving adoption with love and money* (with John Triseliotis and Malcolm Hill, NCB, 1989) and *Freeing children for adoption* (with Maureen Buist, John Triseliotis and Malcolm Hill, BAAF, 1990).

John Triseliotis is Professor of Social Work at Edinburgh University. He has carried out research, taught and lectured in many countries on issues concerned with adoption and foster care. Previous relevant publications include: *In search of origins* (RKP, 1973); editor, *New developments in foster care and adoption* (RKP, 1980); *Hard to place* (with J Russell, Heinemann/ Gower, 1984); editor, *Groupwork in adoption and foster care* (Batsford/ BAAF, 1988); *Achieving adoption with love and money* (with Lydia Lambert and Malcolm Hill, NCB, 1989) and *Freeing children for adoption* (with Lydia Lambert, Maureen Buist and Malcolm Hill, BAAF, 1990).

Contents

Acknowledgements

A study of this kind cannot be undertaken without a great deal of help. It arose from discussions between Family Care, Edinburgh, and the Department of Social Policy and Social Work at the University of Edinburgh. These were followed by consultation with Margaret van Keppel whose generous permission to use and freely adapt the questionnaire used in her Australian study is acknowledged as a major contribution to this work.

From the initial planning stages to the emergence of the final manuscript, the Director and staff of Family Care have given unrestricted access to the appropriate records as well as significant support and encouragement. Members of the Adoption Counselling Team offered their unfailing interest and co-operation throughout the project and these were greatly appreciated. Jean Wallace's administrative help with the study was invaluable. Beatrice Watt typed the manuscript with dedication and infinite patience, sometimes under difficult circumstances.

Computer analysis was expertly undertaken by Lesley Pottie to whom we are particularly grateful for her skill and careful attention to all our requests.

Financial support from the Central Council for Education and Training in Social Work paid the fees for post-graduate student registration at the University of Edinburgh. The Buttle Trust generously agreed to fund the necessary computer analysis and Family Care provided the administrative services essential to every stage of the work.

British Agencies for Adoption & Fostering have made publication possible. We thank them, particularly Christine Hammond and Prue Chennells, for their helpful advice and guidance.

Our warmest appreciation and gratitude are reserved for the birth mothers themselves. Their willingness to share deeply personal experiences of relinquishment with us, sometimes at considerable inconvenience and emotional cost, has been the most important incentive and encouragement.

Patricia Bouchier
Lydia Lambert
John Triseliotis

Foreword

It is sad that the birth of many a child has been accompanied by guilt, shame and the anticipation of long-lasting grief. Those of us who have read this book, in which birth mothers have spoken out in their own words about what it means to give up a child for adoption, have been much moved and have been given cause to reflect on our own practice now and in the past: did we too feel powerless to confront society's punitive attitude, or did we stand by these women and help them to make the best decision for themselves and their children?

Whilst birth mothers were blamed for being poor or torn by conflicting loyalties, little recognition was given to the pain of their predicament. That such pain existed and continued to exist for birth mothers was a fact often either denied or played down by a society with ambivalent attitudes towards women's sexuality and freedom of choice. How ironic that until recently the accepted term for 'birth mother' was 'natural mother': what could be more natural than grieving over the loss of a children?

The Scottish voluntary agency Family Care, which this year celebrates its 80th birthday, had its beginnings in work with women who were at risk of unplanned pregnancy. When it became involved with providing fostering and adoption services, the welfare of birth mothers (and fathers) was not forgotten and in 1984, with the setting up of 'Birth Link', the Adoption Contact Register for Scotland, the commitment to continued care for birth parents was re-confirmed. The research study behind this book therefore derived naturally from Family Care's work, and the agency is pleased to have been able to collaborate in supporting it.

I am delighted, too, to have been given this opportunity to record Family Care's gratitude to the authors for their co-operative and sensitive approach to the research project. In particular, I should mention the importance of the expert contribution of Lydia Lambert in helping with the organisation and presentation of data, enhanced by her own professional experience in helping birth parents and by her patience with a moody computer. Professor John Triseliotis, too, has been a long-standing supporter of Family Care, and brought to the project a breadth of knowledge and understanding in the field of adoption and child care research which is recognised worldwide. For anyone involved with adoption, the ability to listen to birth parents is an essential skill, and for the research study's emphasis on this we must be truly grateful to Pat Bouchier whose strong commitment to the needs of birth parents and respect for their dignity were fundamental to the successful outcome of the project.

Jennifer Speirs,
Director, Family Care
Edinburgh 1991

1 Introduction

Until quite recently, adoption literature has reflected the traditional focus of adoption practice upon adopted people and their adoptive parents. During the past decade, this imbalance has been partially redressed by a number of studies which have recorded the experiences of and assessed the implications for the birth mother who has parted with her child. Not surprisingly, perhaps, most of these studies were based on self-selected samples. The one reported here is no exception.

At the same time, a steady movement towards providing adopted people with the right of access to their personal birth records, and the greater openness in adoption practice itself, have combined to produce significant changes in legislation in most countries where adoption is practised. Based on research carried out in Scotland,[1] the Children Act 1975 (Section 26) gave adopted people in England and Wales opportunities to obtain information about their birth parents similar to those which have been available to their Scottish counterparts since 1930. Elsewhere, notably in New Zealand and some states in Australia and Canada, legislation was planned to include the rights of a birth parent to obtain information about the child who had been relinquished for adoption.

Against this background and following the publicity which was given to the implementation of Section 26 of the Children Act 1975, an increasing number of mothers were encouraged to contact adoption agencies and social services or social work departments throughout Great Britain. For many it was the first time that they had felt able to discuss either their experiences of adoption or the strength of their feelings about the child they had lost. Without specific rights to information or contact, their approaches met with responses which ranged from outright dismissal to concerned acceptance or the offer of individual counselling.

In Edinburgh, Family Care established an adoption counselling and advice centre designed to meet the needs of anyone directly affected by adoption. This independent service frequently received requests for help from birth parents, particularly mothers, and their families seeking either information about a placed child or the opportunity for a meeting. The particular difficulties inherent in their situation were acknowledged and their needs, particularly for emotional support and for information about the adopted child, were addressed in a number of different ways depending on the circumstances.

As a response to growing demand, and in an attempt to fill the widely recognised gap in practical services to both adopted people and their birth families, the official Adoption Contact Register for Scotland, commonly known as Birth Link, was established at Family Care in 1984 with the co-operation and support of the Scottish Office, the Registrar General for Scotland and the Scottish Regional Councils.

In the same year, Robin Winkler and Margaret van Keppel published the results of their Australian survey on the long-term adjustment of relinquishing mothers.[2] The feelings and reactions they reported were of a similar nature and strength to those being expressed to adoption counsellors at Family Care. It was felt that a similar study would be of interest in providing information about birth mothers in Scotland, thus filling a gap in the existing literature on the adoption triangle.

References

1   Triseliotis J *In search of origins* Routledge & Kegan Paul, 1973.

2   Winkler R and van Keppel M *Relinquishing mothers in adoption* Melbourne Institute for Family Studies, 1984.

2 Objectives and method

The main aim of this research was to study the characteristics, personal and social circumstances, motivation, attitudes and current psychological adjustment of mothers who relinquished children for adoption, some of whom may now be seeking contact with them. Basic questions to be asked included:

- What are the effects of relinquishment on the mother?
- What factors make adjustment to relinquishment more or less difficult?
- What distinguishes mothers who wish contact from the rest?

In more detail, the study aimed to:

- examine the influence of a number of variables on the relinquishing mothers' current attitudes to contact, including the quality of perceived counselling received at the time of relinquishment, family or other support and the subjective experience of the loss
- examine these variables, including attitudes to information or contact seeking, or the wish to be protected from such contact, in relation to current physical and psychological health.

The following were some of the hypotheses to be tested:

- The less counselling and family support the mother received at relinquishment over her experience and loss, the more likely it is that she will now be seeking information or reunion rather than showing no interest in either.
- The less counselling and family support the mother received at relinquishment over her experience and loss, the more likely it is that she will be of poorer psychological health, as measured by the General Health Questionnaire (GHQ).[1]

- Unresolved feelings of grief and guilt are likely to correlate with the absence of counselling and wider family support at the time of relinquishment.

- Mothers who recently experienced a personal crisis are likely to be seeking information or a reunion rather than showing no interest in either.

The sample

Forty-nine women who had parted with a child or children for adoption agreed to participate in the study. Each fulfilled the following criteria:

- She had relinquished a child for adoption in Scotland.

- More than eight years had elapsed since relinquishment.

- She had not been involved in a reunion with her child since the adoption was finalised.

- She had volunteered to participate in the study.

- She was available for and agreeable to a personal interview.

- She lived within the geographical area of recruitment.

Recruitment

Most of the mothers were known to Family Care through their registration with Birth Link. All those who had registered between June 1987 and October 1988, and who fulfilled the above criteria, were invited to participate. The remainder were recruited through radio and newspaper publicity. It can be argued that these mothers were the most motivated or that they specially felt the need to share their views and feelings. It is also surmisable that mothers uninterested in contact or in telling their story would be unlikely to respond to a radio and newspaper appeal.

For practical reasons, such as the economical use of the interviewer's travelling time, the need to limit the costs of travel, and the convenience of interviewees, a geographical limit was imposed on the area of recruitment. This covered the central belt of population in Scotland, extending to Ayrshire in the south-west and to Angus in the north-east.

An explanatory letter which outlined the aims of the study and encouraged relinquishing mothers to participate was sent to 56 women. A reply form and a stamped addressed envelope were included, and a reminder was sent if no response had been received within three weeks. Very few reminders were necessary as an immediate and mainly positive response was received, 49 mothers expressing their willingness to be interviewed.

The original aim of the study was to contrast the replies of two main groups of birth mothers: one comprised of those who were eager to make contact with their adopted son or daughter as adults (over the age of 17 years), the other of mothers who were unwilling for contact to take place. Despite various efforts to increase the size of the second group by active recruitment methods, it proved impossible to obtain more than the final five participants.

Sample numbers

Total possible numbers	56
Number of positive responses	49
Trial interviews to test questionnaire	2
Change of mind at interview	1
Final numbers	
contact group, 41	
no-contact group, 5	46

The interview
The interviewer made personal contact with individual mothers as soon as possible to arrange an interview in accordance with the preferences each had expressed in her reply to the introductory letter.

The majority of the interviews were conducted in the home of the relinquishing mother or at another venue in the vicinity. The remainder took place at the offices of Family Care in Edinburgh at the specific request of the interviewee. The interviews were carried out between November 1987 and February 1989.

Each interview was conducted by the same female researcher using a semi-structured questionnaire. The interview itself was conducted in an unstructured and flexible way but ensured that all items on the questionnaire were asked and answered. An initial explanation covering the wider context as well as the specific aims of the study included reassurances on confidentiality and data protection.

The sensitive and potentially distressing nature of the interview was acknowledged, and it was stressed that the needs of the birth mother were the main priority. The time taken to cover the responses to the topics contained in the questionnaire ranged from a minimum of 1½ hours to a maximum of four hours, with an average duration of 2½ hours. The lengthiest interviews were those in which the birth mother was overcome with emotion at recalling the events surrounding the adoption or in describing her present feelings.

All interviews were concluded with an explanation of the planned progress of the study and an offer to forward a summary of the main conclusions once these were available. This offer was accepted with enthusiasm by all participants.

The questionnaire

The semi-structured questionnaire (see appendix) combined a number of closed questions, rating scales and some open-ended questions. The interviewer completed a numbered but unnamed questionnaire for each birth mother. The detailed replies were based on extensive notes taken at the time of the interview. These included quotations from the interviewee's responses to each question wherever possible.

The objectives of the questionnaire were agreed as follows:

– to record the experiences and views of a group of relinquishing mothers in Scotland

– to focus attention on the perceived need expressed by this group of women for any special kind of support to be available at a particular time or times

– to identify any special features of the common sense of loss experienced by the group

– to record the perceived level of adjustment to relinquishment achieved by the birth mothers

– to record attitudes to future contact, with special reference to the operation of Birth Link

– to note any significant implications of Scottish legislation or adoption practice for relinquishing mothers.

The questionnaire was designed to follow the format employed by Winkler and van Keppel.[2] It was divided in the following way:

Section A Demographic information

Section B Pregnancy, confinement and adoption

Section C Post-adoption: reaction and support

Section D Major life events

Section E Current health

Section F Perceived long-term reactions and adjustment

Section G Comments on adoption practice and services past, present and future

Several adjustments were made to the original questionnaire in order to incorporate areas of special interest to the researchers, or to allow for differences between Australian and Scottish adoption legislation and practice. More use was made of open questions to encourage freedom of expression and to elicit detailed responses.

The following are some of the key questions which were added:

Section B the reaction of family and friends to the pregnancy

any specific help available or needed

Section C awareness of the adoption among family and friends

Section D major life events at any time before this pregnancy

any professional assistance with personal difficulties before this pregnancy

Section F awareness of rights and legislation

attitude to support groups or organisations, past and present.

It was also decided to use two supplements (see appendix), one for birth mothers who wished for contact with their child (A) and the other for those who did not (B). Supplement A aimed to record the birth mothers' expectations of the future with particular reference to the use of the facilities associated with Birth Link. It covered the following areas:

information exchange between adopted child and birth parent

– interest in a meeting

– expectations of the future

– attitude to present adoption legislation.

Supplement B was brief, intended mainly to ascertain the influences on the birth mothers' decision and whether there were any circumstances in which this might change. Information was also sought on attitudes to present adoption legislation.

Results
The study obtained vivid accounts of experiences which were still fresh in the minds of most respondents, and these are highlighted in this report. Many of the questions were deliberately framed to encourage these detailed responses, and the frequency with which the main topics were mentioned by the respondents is discussed. These qualitative findings are supported by tables where appropriate.

Data on the current circumstances of all the birth mothers are presented first. The analysis then concentrates on the experiences of mothers who were seeking contact, but refers separately to the no-contact group where relevant.

A few mothers were involved in more than one relinquishment, and their circumstances will sometimes be considered separately from those who spoke about a single experience of adoption.

The main findings have been grouped into chapters or sections representing a chronological sequence of the events experienced by the participants. These sections broadly follow the outline of the questionnaire, but sometimes bring together topics if it is meaningful to look forward to later events or else to refer back from a more recent perspective. This reflects the stance of the birth mothers as they attempted both to describe and to evaluate their situations.

Without a contrast sample of non-relinquishing mothers, it is difficult to say that these characteristics and views are unique to surrendering mothers. That they increase our knowledge and understanding of this particular experience is, however, certain.

References

1   Goldberg D *The detection of psychiatric illness by questionnaire* OUP, 1972.

2   Winkler R and van Keppel M *Relinquishing mothers in adoption* Melbourne Institute for Family Studies, 1984.

3 A demographic profile of the sample

Three of the women in the study were themselves adopted as children. Their particular perspective and views on the experience of relinquishment are reported as appropriate. Several respondents had other contacts with adoption through relatives, partners or friends, but none had become an adoptive parent. All the mothers and the relinquished children were white.

Age and marital status
The majority (35 or 76 per cent) of the 46 relinquishing mothers were more than 35 years of age at the time of the study. Most of them had been in their teens or early twenties when they had given birth to the children (see chapter 4). Over half (28 or 61 per cent) were married or sharing a long-term partnership. Two (4 per cent) were widowed, 12 (26 per cent) were separated or divorced and four (9 per cent) had never been married. The marriages still continued of five of the nine women who had later married the father of the child they re-linquished; the other four were separated or divorced.

Area of residence
Just over one-third of the participants (37 per cent) lived in or near Edinburgh, and as many (37 per cent) were resident in the west of Scotland. This is consistent with the number of birth mothers currently living in Scotland who are registered with Birth Link: 39 per cent are from Lothian Region and 29 per cent from Strathclyde Region.

Occupation
Of the 46 birth mothers in the sample, 31 (67 per cent) were in paid employment at the time of their interview and 15 (33 per cent) were unemployed. Only one woman had never worked outside the home.

Table 1

Present age of birth mothers

Age range	Number	Per cent
27-30	5	11
31-35	6	13
36-40	15	33
41-45	8	17
46-50	6	13
51-60	4	9
Over 60	2	4
Total	46	100

Table 2

Area of residence within Scotland

Area	Number	Per cent
Edinburgh and Lothian	17	37
Glasgow and Strathclyde	17	37
Central	4	9
Fife	4	9
Tayside	4	9
Total	46	100

Present and past employment was used to obtain their occupation groups. Clerical tasks or sales accounted for the largest number (19 or 41 per cent); 25 per cent of the total sample was employed in unskilled or semiskilled jobs. A direct comparison with the relinquishing mothers in the Australian study is not possible because only current occupations were recorded by Winkler and van Keppel.[1] Some similarity in occupational grouping is to be found in the study of a much younger group of birth mothers in Scotland who were earlier interviewed by Triseliotis and Hall.[2]

The same proportion (41 per cent) of clerical occupations occurs. A slightly higher representation in the present study of the managerial/professional group (18 per cent against 11 per cent), together with a lower figure for the skilled and semiskilled manual group (24 per cent to 32 per cent), probably reflects completion of training or promotion by experience in this more mature group of women.

Table 3

Occupational groups

Group	Number	Per cent
Unskilled	7	15
Semiskilled	5	11
Skilled	6	13
Clerical/sales	19	41
Managerial/professional	8	18
Home duties	1	2
Total	46	100

Health and wellbeing

When given an opportunity to record their current state of health, the majority of women considered that their physical health was good or very good. Nine women (20 per cent) had made no visits to their doctor in the last six months and a further 21 (45 per cent) had only been once or twice. The other 15 women (35 per cent) had made more frequent visits to their doctor, including two who were receiving post-operative treatment.

The women's assessment of their emotional health over the past few weeks was ascertained by means of the version of the GHQ having 20 items.[3] This is a screening test which 'detects inability to carry out normal functions, and the appearance of new and distressing phenomena'.[4] It is not a diagnostic tool. The 20-item GHQ has not been divided by its authors into subscales; a later 28-item GHQ was devised for this purpose. We scored the GHQ in two different ways: first, by the same method (1234) as that used by Winkler and van Keppel[5] so that mean scores could be compared; second, by the conventional GHQ method (0011). Whichever method is used, the lower the scores, the better the emotional health of the subjects.

Table 4

Current state of physical health

Physical health	Number	Per cent
Extremely poor	2	4
Poor	6	13
Good	14	31
Very good	19	41
Excellent	5	11
Total	46	100

The first method produced an overall mean score of 43.39. This is slightly higher than the mean score (40.38) obtained by the Australian study.

The majority (70 per cent) of women had low (0–3) scores according to the GHQ method. However, nine mothers revealed scores of 4–9 which indicated that they were experiencing moderate difficulties at the time, while five showed signs (10-15) of more severe emotional problems.

More women (18) scored on the item which asked whether they had 'been feeling unhappy or depressed' than on any other item.

Any number of reasons could have given rise to these feelings, and they could be totally unconnected with the mothers' past experience of relinquishing a child for adoption. However, we examined the

21

possibility that mothers with particularly unhappy memories of that earlier event might also be experiencing current emotional difficulties. These findings are reported in chapter 6.

Table 5

Current state of emotional health

GHQ Score	Number	Per cent
0	10	22
1-3	22	48
4-9	9	19
10-15	5	11
Total	46	100

Table 6

The six items with the highest number of scores

GHQ item	(Respondents with GHQ score = 1 on this item)
Been feeling unhappy or depressed	18
Been taking things hard	14
Been unable to concentrate on whatever you're doing	13
Been thinking of yourself as a worthless person	13
Been feeling nervous and strung up all the time	13
Been losing confidence in yourself	12

Other children
Eight (17 per cent) mothers had no other children besides those relinquished for adoption; 11 (24 per cent) had more children who were full brothers or sisters to those adopted; 27 (59 per cent) had children who would all have been their half-brothers or sisters.

Several mothers had experienced the loss of other children through miscarriage, death or separation, which had compounded their feelings about the relinquished children.

Information relating to the adopted child

A total of *51 children* were involved because four mothers had relinquished more than one child (three children in one case and two in three cases). Another mother, who had also had two children adopted, chose to concentrate on just one of these adoptions. Twenty-nine (57 per cent) of the children were males and 22 (43 per cent) females. One child was placed twice with an interval of two years due to changes of mind. Thus, *52 placements* for adoption were experienced by the mothers in the study.

Forty (77 per cent) of the placements had been made when the children were less than six months old, and 47 (90 per cent) children altogether were surrendered within the first year of birth. At the time when their mothers were interviewed, their ages ranged from 10 to 39, with an average (mean) of 19 years. The majority (76 per cent) were over the age when they could in Scotland legally begin the process of searching for their birth parents.

Views about contact

As already indicated in chapter 2, most of the birth mothers in this study were themselves actively seeking contact with their adopted children, and all but two of these 41 women had registered with Birth Link. They formed the *contact group*. Three mothers in this group wished to contact more than one child, and the mother whose child had been placed on two separate occasions was also seeking contact. More of the children in this group were boys (58 per cent).

There were five mothers who were not seeking contact and they formed the *no-contact group*. One of these mothers related her experiences of relinquishing two children. There were equal numbers of boys and girls in this group.

References

1   Winkler R and van Keppel M *Relinquishing mothers in adoption* Melbourne Institute for Family Studies, 1984.

2   Triseliotis J and Hall E 'Giving consent to adoption' *Social work today* 2 17, 1971.

3   Goldberg D *The detection of psychiatric illness by questionnaire* OUP, 1972.

4   Goldberg D and Williams P *User's guide to the General Health Questionnaire* NFER Nelson, 1988.

5   See 1 above.

4 Pregnancy and confinement

The memories of their pregnancy and confinement were inextricably bound up with the process of relinquishment which followed immediately afterwards for all but two of the birth mothers in our sample. Both these mothers had their children placed for adoption against their wishes several years later. However, like the others, they had been single or unsupported when their children were born. Mothers of 40 (87 per cent) of the children were unmarried at the time of relinquishment and 11 (23 per cent) were separated, widowed or divorced.

Major events before pregnancy

Even though most of the mothers were still in their teens or early twenties when they became pregnant, many of them had already experienced major crises or developments in their lives. Only a few recalled important events of a generally positive nature. Three major categories of experience emerged:

- an insecure childhood or young adulthood (119 references)

- death or loss (20 references)

- positive experiences (17 references)

Insecure childhood

These experiences were characterised by: poor relationships with or between parents or their partners; adherence to strict moral or religious codes of behaviour; the social deprivation of poverty; alcoholism, sometimes associated with domestic violence; sexual abuse; single parenthood.

> Throughout my childhood my parents' marriage was violent and unstable. My mother was emotionally detached and rejecting.

> I had a miserable childhood. We were tied to chairs so that we couldn't get up to mischief.

25

When I was six some friends told me that I was adopted. I did not believe them and could not understand why my parents had kept it a secret. They were both in and out of mental hospitals. I had to sign them out several times when I was in my teens. My father eventually committed suicide when I was 16, dying of an overdose in my arms.

For six years, from the age of 11 to 17 years, I was sexually abused by a man down the stairs. My mother must have known but she kept sending me on messages to him even when I pleaded with her not to.

It was a religious, god-fearing childhood. I was materially spoiled and my parents were loving in their own way, but they could not show deep feelings and subjects like sex were never discussed.

I was married at 18 and had my first child at 20. I left my first husband because I felt trapped in an early marriage.

Death or loss
This event involved members of the family or close friends and included experiences of separation both as a child and as an adult.

My mother died when I was three and I was sent away to an aunt in England. My father remarried and I was never close to my step-mother. I wanted to stay with my grandmother but they just moved me from place to place. I had four changes of primary school. I just hated my life and never felt part of the family.

When I was 15 my father died. He and I were very close. All my mother could find to say to me was 'your behaviour killed your father'. I lost not only him but, because there was less money, I missed the opportunity to stay on at school and go to university.

My mother had to work when I went to school and she was too busy to respond to a child's needs for her time and affection. When my father died I was 11 and, apart from being greatly affected by his loss, I completely lost touch with my mother because she had to work even harder.

When my father took ill, my sister-in-law moved into the house and just took over. Although I was 15 and capable, they did not let me help. My mother did not tell me my father was dying and he had to ask for me to go to the hospital. I still feel dreadful about that.

Positive experiences
These refer to childhood, personal relationships and early adult life:

My childhood was happy and secure, if poor. We had a strict Church of Scotland upbringing according to a rigid moral code. There was little freedom or independence, though.

I was a high achiever at school, good at everything and head girl. My father was so proud.

When asked whether they had received any assistance with personal problems before the pregnancy which resulted in parting with a child, only a handful of mothers recalled receiving social work intervention. This was mainly with difficulties arising from single parenthood, emotional instability or alcoholism in the family.

Others would have liked help but did not receive it and their difficulties remained unresolved. As one mother observed: 'Because of the difficulties in my relationship with my mother, I was inclined to brood and was much too easily hurt'.

Social and family attitudes to pregnancy
The majority of the children (61 per cent) were surrendered for adoption between 1961 and 1970. Their parents' experiences reflect the changes which were taking place in relationships between young men and women during the 1960s, and demonstrate some of the anomalies which arose when society's attitudes and responses lagged behind these developments in some respects. Many of the traditional attitudes persisted until much later.

In a survey of 1,873 teenagers interviewed during the early years of the decade, Michael Schofield[1] established that, by the age of 18 years, 34 per cent of the boys and 17 per cent of the girls were sexually experienced, but 16 per cent of boys and 18 per cent of girls knew nothing about birth control; many others only had a slight knowledge of contraceptives. The young women invariably relied on their partners to undertake full responsibility. Access to advice and practical help with birth control for unmarried partners was severely restricted during this time.

Many of the boys (40 per cent) were unconcerned about pregnancy and, although more girls expressed fear of becoming pregnant, they did little about prevention. Many boys expressed a traditional expectation that they would marry a pregnant girlfriend, and this appeared to coincide with what the girls hoped would occur.

Despite the views on marriage expressed in that survey, a study of the Registrar General's statistics since 1938 on rates of illegitimacy and pre-marital conception showed that a rise in the illegitimacy rate was accompanied by a drop in the percentage of pregnant teenage brides. It was concluded, therefore, that the social pressure on single pregnant women to marry had declined.

In this study of relinquishing mothers in Scotland, few mentioned pressure to marry the father of the child as a significant factor, although many felt let down and rejected by him. Several commented on the very different response they would have received from their parents if they had planned to marry; much personal criticism and abuse derived from the birth mother's refusal to marry under these circumstances. Some birth fathers also resisted the pressure of parents or refused to accept responsibility for the pregnancy; others showed deep concern but were refused access to the birth mother by the adults in control of her living situation.

Table 7

Main reactions of family to pregnancy of birth mother

Response	Number	Per cent
Hurt, upset	10	20
Angry, shamed by social stigma	27	53
Physical or verbal abuse	4	8
Qualified acceptance	10	19
Total	51	100

In Schofield's survey,[2] each of the girls had been asked what she would do in the event of becoming an unmarried mother. All expressed a wish to keep the child. Neither adoption nor abortion (not legalised until the Abortion Act 1967) were favoured by the teenage girls. There is of course a difference between intentions and actual behaviour, and many of the women in this study believed they were forced to face reality at the time of the pregnancy and birth. Single mothers during the 1960s had to be prepared to deal with strong social and personal censure. The stigma of giving birth outside marriage was a harsh reality for them as well as for their children, and stigma emerged as the reaction of their family and friends to the pregnancy most frequently mentioned by the mothers.

Families themselves were critical, often against a strong moral or religious background, and some used physical or uncontrolled verbal abuse.

> My parents would not consider helping me to keep her. They could have but the stigma was too much for them and me and the baby at that time.

> I saw them for what they really were – self-righteous, afraid and not the forgiving Christian parents that they pretended to be.

> I never felt there was anything to be ashamed of but they did.

> I was helpless against all their anger and abuse.

> They were so ashamed that they just totally rejected me; my mother would actually pass me in the street without a word.

> I had to leave my home, my job, my friends because they were so ashamed.

> Horror – everything must be hidden from friends and neighbours. The one or two who knew would use a special signal on the front door so that I did not have to go and hide in my room.

> Only my mother knew. She made me pack my bags as soon as I told her and it was three years before we spoke again. She was absolutely terrified of the scandal. She has never referred to the incident since that time and nor have I.

> My father was furious. There were no visits, no contact in hospital, no discussions about the baby. It was as though the whole thing had never happened.

> My father beat me to teach me a lesson.

> They tried to find an abortionist for me, then made me try all the home remedies to cause a miscarriage. It often worries me that this could have harmed the baby.

Even those parents who showed sympathy and understanding of their daughter's predicament felt the stigma connected with having a baby outside marriage. The shame of an unmarried pregnancy in the family often proved too great a threat for them to handle.

> The family were shocked and upset but understanding, although there was never any real prospect of their helping me to keep her. They just waited until I had 'come round' to the idea of adoption.

> They were angry at first but then gave me lots of support, hoping I would let my mother or one of my sisters adopt the baby and keep the whole thing a family secret.

Age of mother at child's birth

Despite an overall age range of 14 to 48 years, the majority (43 or 84 per cent) of births took place when the relinquishing mothers were under 25 years old.

Table 8

Age at child's birth

Age	Number	Per cent
14–16 years	8	16
17–19 years	21	41
20–24 years	14	27
25–29 years	5	10
30–39 years	0	0
Over 40 years	3	6
Total	51	100

In their study of decision-making in giving consent to adoption, Triseliotis and Hall[3] also found that 'the under 25 age group predominated'. However, a smaller proportion than in the present study (36 per cent compared with 57 per cent) were under 20 years of age. In observing that age did not appear to have a direct bearing on the decision to keep or relinquish their baby, Triseliotis and Hall stated that it was 'certainly not the under 20 age group who were more likely to surrender their babies'. They also suggested that the youngest mothers 'took time to internalise the pregnancy' and may also have been 'unable to take a decision independent of their parents'.

Both these factors emerged as important influences in the present study. It was possible that the long-term emotional effects of an early pregnancy and relinquishment, together with pressure to choose adoption against the true instincts and feelings of the teenage mother, produced a major impact on her attitude to future contact with the relinquished child. All but a few of the mothers in this study had taken the positive step of registering their interest on Birth Link. Unlike the earlier study, where two mothers aged over 40 'felt they were too old', none of the three mothers from this age group in our study gave their age as a reason for relinquishment. In one of these cases, the child was not placed for adoption until several years later.

Living situation
The realisation that they were pregnant raised difficult questions for these women about where to live during this time, especially towards the end when their condition became more obvious. At the time of the birth, mothers of 17 (33 per cent) of the children were living with their parents, 15 (30 per cent) were resident in Mother and Baby Homes and 19 (37 per cent) were living with relatives or independently.

A few mothers concealed their pregnancy, and one of them described how her family 'had to cope with the shock when I was rushed into hospital'. Others who stayed at home with their parents were severely restricted or were subjected to rude comments if they went out.

It was a very unhappy time because my parents quarrelled even more about me and made it clear I was the black sheep. I was not allowed to show myself outside and was locked in my room when people came to the house.

My parents eventually got over their shock and anger and looked after me. Although I had to put up with small boys calling me 'pregnant cow', there was no problem from neighbours and friends.

Slightly less than half the mothers moved away from their home community during their pregnancy. Some went to live with relatives or friends.

> I was quite alone until a friend helped me to run away to her mother who had five other children. My own mother just shouted, shouted and condemned me.

> My married sister and her husband took me in and we became even closer.

Others had already left home because of difficulties there; for some, pregnancy increased their moves from the proverbial pillar to post.

> I had already left home due to physical abuse by my adoptive mother and was homeless in Glasgow. Then a friend's family gave me shelter but I left when I knew I was pregnant because I could not upset them when they had been good to me. The Mother and Baby Home was a nightmare.

Until society's attitudes towards unmarried mothers and single parents gradually became more accepting, it was common for many younger mothers to be sent to Mother and Baby Homes. One described how she felt 'sent away and abandoned, hidden away... because I was so bad'.

For some the institution was 'a refuge. I had taken an overdose before I was sent there and they were kindness itself'. The friendship and help offered by other residents could also provide solace.

> I was the youngest in the home (14 years) and I will always remember the kindness of two older girls who cared for and protected me.

> The other girls were a great help. It was good to know you were not alone in the situation. I made a good friend and we shared everything.

However, several mothers were less fortunate and recalled harsh memories of this experience.

> I felt out of place. I hated the way the other girls behaved and

spoke, especially about men. I was very quiet and immature and they frightened me.

They said nothing to me, did not tell me where I was going or what would happen. They refused to let the baby's father know where I was but I phoned him and he came. The matron threatened us but we went and sat in Princes Street Gardens in the cold and just cried together.

It was an awful place, all rules and chores and regulations. No free time to speak of except for two hours in the evening. But I am grateful to them. Where else could I have gone?

The hostel was run by a dreadful woman – judgemental, moralistic, snobbish. It was all 'them and us' because some of the girls were of a lower social class than I was. The committee woman who visited was a patronising do-gooder who did a tour of the place on her charity morning. I met somebody with the same name later and could hardly speak to her I was so full of hate.

Some of the mothers' bitterest comments involved the lack of understanding which they felt had been shown towards them by those in charge of homes over decisions about the child.

The matron was unmarried, unsympathetic and refused to help me obtain one of their flats so that I could keep the baby. Nobody was available to talk to or to make contact with the baby's father and his family for me.

There was no question of caring for the mothers themselves. The place was regimented and emotionally cold. One incident stays in my mind for its cruelty. On the day I left I was taken round all the girls who had kept their babies. This was straight after I had left my baby in the hospital in a complete daze and was on my way back home.

The hospital experience
Experiences of community medical and hospital services were of particular importance to this group of mothers, many of whom told us they had had no previous experience of admission to hospital. Preparation for childbirth in the form of ante-natal care or classes did not seem to have been offered to the majority. Ignorance and fear were prevalent, especially among the younger mothers.

It was dreadful. I had no idea what was going to happen and I was terrified. All they could do was smack me when I screamed. Nobody suggested a painkiller.

It was so impersonal – a horrific experience. I was left alone completely, the longest night, totally abandoned and wishing it was all over.

I remember being relieved when they said he would arrive later than I thought. I was holding that baby in for as long as possible, absolutely terrified of having him and having to give him up.

Why couldn't somebody have been with me at the birth – my mother or sister or the baby's father even though we weren't married?

Of the hospital service itself, mothers of 26 (51 per cent) of the children expressed themselves as not at all satisfied, 14 (27 per cent) were moderately satisfied and 11 (22 per cent) considered themselves completely satisfied with the care they received. More negative than positive comments (3:1) were recorded on the response received from hospital staff. Only two mothers mentioned a visit from a hospital social worker and the majority did not see their adoption agency worker between admission to hospital and discharge into the community.

I remember almost nothing. I have blotted out whole bits of it. Nobody came to tell me about the baby. I thought 'he is not mine at all, I cannot even ask about him'. It was as though you were being punished.

You weren't yourself at all. They spoke about you but never with you.

The main thing missing was instruction about childbirth and caring for the child. The baby was premature and very difficult to feed. They kept criticising but gave me no help or reassurance.

The baby was their only concern.

I broke my heart in the toilets but put on a mask outside. Surely they must have noticed that I needed help.

I had to return to a ward full of mothers and their new babies. It was very cruel.

Despite the preponderence of negative comments, some mothers recalled actions which minimised the problems associated with their particular situation and made the hospital experience more tolerable.

> I was just called 'Mrs' and no difference made. I was a mother like everyone else and didn't have the plague. I did not feel any stigma or criticism.

> They gave me a choice in everything and encouraged my family to visit.

> The nurses were wonderful. They put me back into the ante-natal ward – very thoughtful. Some of them came round to chat to me and they were very willing to listen.

Contact with child in hospital

One in four of the children (13) was not seen at all by the mother after birth, and almost the same number (12 or 24 per cent) were only viewed through the window of the hospital nursery. The rest (26 or 51 per cent) were held and usually fed by their mothers.

Personal choice over whether to see or care for their babies was open to mothers in some hospitals but not in others. These findings are in accordance with those recorded by Triseliotis and Hall.[4] Where there was a possibility of adoption, it was common practice to keep the child and the mother apart.

> They just told me what I was going to do – no discussion, no choice, just 'you won't be able to see the baby'.

> They actually held up a blanket in front of me to cover the baby when he was born in case I got a glimpse. But you can't pretend it hasn't happened. It only hits you harder later on when all you've got is your fantasies.

Mothers who were compelled to abide by the rules of the hospital or adoption agency against their wishes experienced increased tension or anxiety and appeared to have more regrets.

> I just wish I could have satisfied myself that he was all right – counted his fingers and toes.

> Why didn't I insist on seeing her and looking after her? It would have given me some good things to remember. There aren't any others. But I just wasn't brave enough to stand up to them.

One had faced great opposition in order to do what she felt was best for her child.

> Sister was a real dragon. She made me feel very guilty, saying I had no right to see or feed the baby if I was not going to keep him but I knew I was doing the right thing for him.

However, another mother, who had accepted that it would be best not to see her baby, suddenly found herself having to care for the child because of staff shortages in the hospital. She described her feelings and the consequences which led to changes of mind and two placements for adoption.

> Those ten days nearly drove me mad. You try not to become attached but there is no way out. It made me ask for her back after she had gone to the new parents and she was unsettled and unhappy until she was finally adopted at the age of four.

Mothers who were able to make a choice about caring for the child expressed fewer regrets than those who were forced to accept the hospital's regime. Nevertheless, some of them recalled very mixed feelings about whether they had made the right decision.

> I cared for him for two weeks but I have no regrets. I wanted to give him everything even though I knew it was best he should be adopted.

> Caring for her made me face up to things – I am very good at not facing things until I have to. I could not have made the decision any other way.

> My only regret about caring for him was that I couldn't keep him. He is my only child and I am glad I was able to care for him myself for a little while even if the parting was made even more painful.

> I knew if I saw her I could not go through with the adoption. I regret this now because I have nothing to remember her by.

The choice was a particularly painful one for a mother who already had another child.

> It was a mistake not to handle and feed her. I just didn't dare because I could not bring up two children. But I should have. That would have been the right thing to do.

Naming the child

The mothers usually registered their babies in their own surname. Just one child was registered in his birth father's name by parents who later married. Many relinquishing mothers commented on the importance attached to the choice of first names, using the opportunity to bestow upon their child a particular favourite or ones with special significance. Several mentioned how upset they were to discover, often years later, that first names as well as surnames were usually changed by adoption.

> It removed my last link with her, the only thing I felt I had given her that would last.

> I don't know how to think about him now. He was always 'Robert' to me.

References

1   Schofield M *The sexual behaviour of young people* Longman, 1965.

2   See 1 above.

3   Triseliotis J and Hall E 'Giving consent to adoption' *Social work today* 2 17, 1971.

4   See 3 above.

5 The decision to relinquish

The decision to part with a child is never easy. The majority of mothers in our sample faced this choice over their first-born child (35 or 69 per cent) but 13 (25 per cent) of the 51 children were second born and 3 (6 per cent) were third or later children. One mother experienced the removal of all three of her children at the same time, when they were aged from 5 to 10 years. The others who parted with a second- or later-born child all made this decision in the first weeks or months after the birth. Three mothers spoke to us about relinquishing both their first- and second-born children, while 11 described situations where their decisions had to take into account the rearing of at least one other child.

Twelve of the 14 second- or later-born children who were relinquished soon after birth were born between 1962 and 1970. Although attitudes towards single parents were changing during this period, the practical difficulties of coping alone were considerable, particularly the economic deprivations resulting from dependence on state benefits or else on low paid and often part-time work.[1]

Many mothers who tried to work were thwarted by difficulties in finding and paying for adequate childminding facilities. Day nurseries were too few or too remote. A Scottish study of mothers bringing up children on their own drew attention to the expense of day care, travel and meals for a woman working full time.[2] Maternity benefit was available only to those who had contributed for one to two years previously.

Marsden[3] established that a shortage of bed space occurred in one in ten families; bed sharing of an adult and two children was common practice. Single mothers who gained council houses did so only through exceptional support from welfare authorities, doctors, health visitors or disability self-help groups. Many housing authorities were reluctant to allocate accommodation to fatherless families because they represented a poor economic risk. The emotional effects of trying to bring up children single handed also took their toll. Many parents lived in fear that their children might be taken into care.[4]

Influences in reaching a decision

Against this background, it was not unexpected to find that economic pressures influenced the majority of the birth mothers in the present study at the time when they were considering adoption. In nearly a third of the 52 placements, a lack of financial resources was given as the main reason for surrendering the child for adoption. In a further 19 per cent, mothers felt that their single status, with its implicit lack of practical support and financial independence, was the major factor in making the decision. The wishes of parents, many of whom were unable to support a single mother and her child in a family with average or low income, was the major factor given for another 21 per cent of placements.

> It was impossible for me to cope on my own. There was no money unless I worked.

> My parents both worked and we had little money. I could not ask them to support me and another child or my mother to stay at home while I worked.

> I would have been homeless if I had kept the baby because my parents had no room.

Table 9

Main reasons for adoption

Reason	Number	Per cent
Financial	16	31
Wishes of parents	11	21
Single status	10	19
Too young	9	17
Child in care of local authority	3	6
Other	3	6
Total	52*	100

One of the 51 children had two placements: see chapter 3.

Many of the mothers said they had spent a great deal of time during the intervening years reflecting on the decision to surrender their child for adoption. Even those who felt that the decision had been the right one at the time recognised the strength of the external pressures, particularly those which occurred within their own families. They emphasised the degree of dependence of young people on their parents, the restrictions placed upon them, and the lack of preparation for adult life which was felt, either at the time or in retrospect, to have been a major factor in the final outcome.

Whether or not they gave the attitude of their parents as the major reason for relinquishing their child, the majority of the women felt it to be an important influence on their situation.

> If I had kept the child, I would have to have lived at home and my mother would have taken over. I was and am so critical of my own upbringing with all its restrictions that I simply could not allow that to happen to my child.

> They had always been too strict, never discussed anything but just laid down the law.

> My parents refused absolutely to stand by me and help me bring up their grandchild.

> They simply took over and organised everything without telling me. I cannot understand now why I did not stand up to them.

These findings make an interesting comparison with those of Triseliotis and Hall[5] who interviewed birth mothers within a few months of relinquishment. They found that 'complex family pressures' appeared to influence over half of the mothers who confided in their parents. Confirmation of some of the above quotations may be found in the observation by the previous researchers that their group of mothers 'made it sound as if their own wishes and outlook coincided with those of their parents'. Raynor[6] also referred to the attitude 'or supposed attitude' of their parents as one of the four reasons most often given for considering adoption by unmarried mothers. With the advantages of a period of reflection, greater emotional maturity and disengagement from the influence of their parents, the birth mothers in the present study were able to give a more penetrating insight into the complex factors at work. Nevertheless, they may also have learned to rationalise the reasons for relinquishment to help deal with feelings of guilt or doubt.

For birth parents whose relationship as a couple was important to them and who earnestly sought ways of caring for their child, the feelings of sadness and frustration amounted to desperation at times.

> I was 14 when the first baby was born and a year older the second time. Because I was under age, I was terrified of the police, afraid their father would be put in jail and me with him. We loved each other but were helpless until he got a divorce, but by then it was too late. My parents just shouted and condemned; they only cared about their own shame and disgrace. But the joke was that everybody knew. They could have helped but they just condemned me.

Other young birth parents confirmed the difficulties facing them.

> There was no way we could support ourselves as school leavers let alone give adequate care to a baby.

> We were completely trapped and unable to find a way out of the darkness. Years later his sister said she would have helped us if she had known.

> We were very happy about the baby and I really enjoyed the pregnancy but we were 17. It never dawned on us that we wouldn't manage.

Some mothers were contemplating marriage to men who were not their child's father and felt it was best not to jeopardise this new relationship by bringing the baby into it. Other mothers sincerely felt that their child would be better off with 'two parents who really wanted her', especially if they were already bringing up one child and were 'afraid that both children would be deprived'. One mother in the no contact group was frank that she had 'resented' the baby and wanted to continue her job, while another admitted that she had no maternal feelings for children.

One dilemma which could have made the adoption decisions even more difficult did not affect this group of mothers: none of the children was reported to have had any disabilities. At least one baby had been very premature and had been kept in hospital, but all the children were considered 'suitable for adoption' on medical grounds.

Feelings about the relinquishment decision

In just over a third of the decisions, mothers felt that the adoption was in accordance with their own wishes. Many qualified their replies by stating that this decision was taken in the best interests of the child.

I was determined to do my best by both of my children.

It was what I thought was best at the time. I was glad he was going to a good home.

I was uncertain about my ability to be a good mother. Adoption was a great relief – the best thing for me and the child.

Because I was adopted myself, I thought I knew what was best.

Table 10

Degree to which adoption based on mothers' wishes

Degree	Number	Per cent
Completely as wanted	18	35
Moderately as wanted	11	21
Not at all as wanted	23	44
Total	52	100

In 11 instances, the mothers felt that the adoption was only partially what they wanted, usually because no alternative to adoption presented itself as a solution.

I was helpless. It was the only chance given me.

It was like being caught in a trap and struggling to get free.

It was an impossible situation. Adoption was the only way forward but it was totally against my feelings.

There was no other solution. I had to tell myself he would not have to suffer as I had done by living in my parents' home.

In nearly half of the adoptions, the mothers considered that the decision was not at all what they wanted. Even at the time, they could see nothing positive in making this decision.

I always believed it would never happen, that somehow I would get him back.

I loved children and hated the thought of what I was doing.

It was forced on me by my father.

I did not make the decision. It was made for me.

It was hardly surprising that one of those who felt that the adoption decision had been 'not at all as wanted' was the mother with three children.

It was completely against my wishes. I had asked them (social work department) to take the three children into care for a few weeks to let me get back on my feet after all the problems. Then it seemed to happen like the click of your fingers. They didn't tell me about the adoption. It was my daughter. I couldn't believe the social worker had discussed it with the children and not me. I said to the head supervisor, 'It's as if he doesn't want me to get them back – he wasn't going to help me in any way'.

Placement for adoption and the role of the adoption worker

The majority of the placements were undertaken by voluntary or private adoption agencies (65 per cent) and the remainder were organised by local authority children's or social work departments (35 per cent). Although most of the women were referred to a placing agency at some stage during their pregnancy, few could recall having more than one or two contacts with a social worker. Opportunities for pre-adoption counselling or individual discussion were remembered by only seven (14 per cent) of the women, five of whom regarded this as being of some help to them.

The circumstances of the actual day on which they parted with their baby were recalled with pain and distress by most of the mothers. The majority were able to remember the event in considerable detail even when the separation had taken place nearly 40 years previously. Others had difficulty recalling the facts with any accuracy. This caused them considerable distress and guilt, but they were able to recognise that they had needed to protect themselves from the intense pain experienced at the time of their loss.

For those who had cared for their children in hospital or at home, or who had kept contact during the period of fostering which preceded the adoption placement, the separation was particularly stressful. In some cases, the actual timing of the parting was withheld from these birth mothers. This effectively prevented them from 'saying a proper goodbye' and intensified their feelings of rejection and exclusion. Others left their babies in hospital without seeing them after their own discharge, or were told later that their children had been removed to foster care at approximately the same time.

The emotional distress of relinquishment was frequently increased by a perceived failure of adoption workers to respond to the birth mothers' wish to retain a tangible link. Those who sent gifts which were well received and acknowledged by a letter of thanks from adoptive parents, or who received a progress report from the agency itself, or whose request for a photograph was successful, spoke warmly of the benefits these brought. A positive response appeared to reassure them that their children would be told about their mothers' concern and affection for them. Later, when they began to have fears that their child might not be told about being adopted, these early exchanges helped to persuade them that the truth would be told.

The majority of relinquishing mothers found that their daily lives and wellbeing were profoundly affected at the time of placement. Three recalled receiving regular support from the adoption worker, and these mothers felt that some recognition of their own needs was being made. Another mentioned her family doctor as being 'really wonderful – a kind and sensible lady'. A few others had been helped by the foster mother, their minister or solicitor, or had joined a group for single parents. However, it was far more common to remember post-relinquishment contact as being confined to formal communication from the adoption agency, often by letter, on the question of arrangements for signing consent to the adoption. From the birth mothers' point of view, these contacts appeared to focus on the legal and practical issues. They did not consider that any significant attempt had been made to respond to their own situation except as it concerned the baby's placement.

Two out of three mothers could not recall receiving any other assistance soon after they had placed their child for adoption. One or two of them said they did not know who to go to or how to ask for help, but the rest simply had no memories of assistance at this time.

Giving consent to adoption
The studies by Triseliotis and Hall[7] and Raynor[8] were commissioned

by the Houghton Committee specifically to enquire into the timing and finality of giving consent to adoption as changes to the existing legislation were being considered. Only eight placements (15 per cent) in the present study took place after these changes came into effect in 1976. So most of the mothers in it experienced the same procedures under the Adoption Act of 1958 as mothers in the earlier studies, with very similar results. However, one child was placed shortly before changes introduced by the previous Adoption Act of 1950, and his mother had been asked twice to give her consent. She still remembered the second time as 'particularly painful'.

> It eats your heart out but I could not go back on it then – what about the adoptive parents?

Table 11

Whether birth mother signed consent form

Consent signed	Number	Per cent
Yes	43	83
No	6	11
Do not remember	3	6
Total	52	100

In the majority of adoptions, mothers said they had signed the consent form. In three cases they could not remember, but in six adoptions the consent form was not signed. One of these refusals involved the child who was later placed for adoption for a second time (with consent). Her mother gave a description of these events which made clear the contrasts between the circumstances of each adoptive placement, the way they were handled and their effect on her willingness to give consent.

> From the start my parents wanted me to keep my baby and leave it in their care but I would not consider this as they were such poor parents themselves. Then in the hospital I had to care for her for ten days although I was told I wouldn't have to do this. Perhaps if bonding had never started I would not have changed my mind later.

45

The adoption agency made arrangements for a couple to receive my daughter but after four hours these were cancelled.

I thought, 'these people do not really want my baby. It is just like sending an old coat, an unwanted coat to a jumble sale'. Then they found different parents for her but I got no information, there was no contact at all. So on the day of signing the consent I changed my mind and returned home with her. But I was forced to leave her with my parents while I worked and just before her second birthday they quarrelled and told the social work department to take her into care. I was only informed afterwards.

I had no proper home for her and she was so unhappy. The social worker said the child should be settled very soon, so for two years she lived with a family with a view to adoption. This time the social worker kept in touch to give me progress reports and to reassure me. She knew just how I was feeling and I was included in the plans until the adoption was granted. They encouraged me to let them know if I ever changed my address.

When those who had signed their consent were asked if they had considered changing their minds later on, three out of five said 'no'. These included all the mothers in the no contact group. However, many mothers in both groups made comments to the effect that they felt they had 'no alternative' to going through with the adoption. Most claimed that they had not been told they could change their minds after signing. One or two had delayed signing their consent but then held to their decision, while others made comments which showed that they were aware of the prospective adopters' feelings.

Why should I be that rotten? I knew somebody who had adopted a child, and until it was final she was a nervous wreck.

Concern for the adopters, as well as for their child, also lay behind the decision not to withdraw consent of several of the 18 mothers who considered changing their minds.

I couldn't take him away from his new parents. I simply couldn't do that.

It would not have been fair to her or the new parents. No good causing even more heartbreak than I had.

A lot of thought went into it . . . I felt they had earned the right to keep him after all those weeks.

In more than half the cases where mothers said they had considered changing their minds, they had not felt like giving consent all along but could not see a way out.

I was never sure about it, because I really wanted to keep her but I was shown no way to do this.

I was unhappy about losing him from the beginning but there was no other way.

Others had been affected by changes in their circumstances after the placement, which made them wonder whether to ask for their child back. This was especially likely if they were reunited with the birth father, or if their own parents showed signs of relenting. One mother went to live with two single parents who had kept their children. She got as far as writing to the adoption agency but decided not to ask for her baby to be returned to her as this would have been an 'inhuman thing to do to child and parents'. Another mother described the scene when she visited the adoption agency with the intention of declaring her change of mind:

I sat down in her office and – I'm sure it was a put-up job – there was an ashtray full of cigarette butts on the desk, and she said she'd just been trying to console a couple whose baby had been returned to a mother who'd changed her mind. I just felt deflated and couldn't say what I'd come to say: 'I want my baby back'.

There were also examples of implicit or explicit pressure from families to sign their consent:

When it came to signing I thought: 'I can't do this to them (my parents) after they've tried to keep everything so quiet and paid for the home etc.'

I realise now that the second pregnancy was almost getting back at my parents for not letting me keep the first baby, their own grandchild. Did I think things would be different next time? My mother knew what was going through my mind, but on the way to sign the papers she threatened me with being thrown out and earning my living on the streets if I said I was being forced to sign.

Some mothers discussed the possibility of changing their minds with everyone they could think of – social workers, parents, relatives, the birth father or new partners – but one in three kept their uncertainty to themselves and discussed the situation with nobody else.

Satisfaction with the way the adoption was handled
When asked to sum up their feelings about the way the adoption was handled, mothers responded that they were satisfied with one in four of the placements. In two cases they replied 'yes and no', but generally mothers expressed dissatisfaction (71 per cent) with the way in which the adoption was handled.

The mothers who were satisfied expressed their appreciation of the adoption workers' acceptance of their feelings, the practical help with arrangements and explanations about adoption procedure. Several commented that they were just wanting it to be over at the time but now wished they had been given more information. Others felt they had been helped to understand the implications of adoption in a way which influenced their final decision. Those who were dissatisfied often maintained that the adoption agency had exercised a powerful but biased influence over their decision to relinquish the child. Advice had tended to concentrate on the advantages of adoption and little attempt was made to examine the alternatives in a constructive way.

> I needed to talk to somebody neutral about the options, the decisions and the future – how it would affect me.

> It was their elitist attitude towards adoption that I resented. Just because adopters have money and position does not make them good parents. I know that now. At the time nobody suggested to me that I could be a good mother but I have been.

> You just become resigned to the inevitable.

> As professionals they should have been less prejudiced. They took a particular stand instead of providing opportunities for discussion.

Many of the youngest mothers considered they were given no opportunities for discussion on their own without the presence of one or both parents.

My mother was always there. How could I speak freely about what I really felt?

I needed support in standing up to my parents. Instead I felt they were in collusion with my parents against me.

Once again there was much criticism of the neglect of the birth mothers' own needs. One mother commented that 'it was all in the baby's best interest' and many others considered they had been deliberately made to feel that any course other than adoption would have been further proof of their irresponsibility and 'badness'.

I needed somebody to help me feel better about myself and permission to say what I felt.

It was the attitude towards the birth mother that was so unhelpful. They only seemed to be interested in a healthy baby to hand over.

I wish I had had a better relationship with the adoption worker. I found her to be distant and difficult to talk to. There were many questions I wanted to ask but I even felt guilty asking about my baby.

It was all so rushed. I felt I needed longer to find an alternative and to make up my mind what the best thing was to do.

I needed much more information on the adoption procedure. I never knew I could have changed my mind and I have discovered that we were married before the adoption order was granted.

In their own view and that of practically everyone around them, the women felt they had little to offer a baby and there was no difficulty in presenting adoption to them in a favourable light. Their own instincts were 'to do everything I possibly could to make up for having to give him away'. However, the fact that these ambitions were in direct conflict with their maternal feelings produced strong and often angry reactions against the neglect and rejection which were perceived to be the response of adoption workers.

I needed to meet and talk with the adoptive parents. They took my baby and knew all about me but I know absolutely nothing about them.

I was suffering terribly because I had lost him. Eventually I phoned and they said I could have a photo but it never came. I wanted to let the new parents know myself how much I cared so they could tell him about me and pass it on to him.

They told me I would soon get over it but how do you live with giving up your baby?

The degree of satisfaction with the help of the adoption worker recorded by the mothers in this study is far lower than that obtained by Triseliotis and Hall[9] who reported that eight out of ten mothers felt the social workers were helpful or partly helpful. It is reasonable to suppose that in the early stages of relinquishment, the value of practical support, of guidance through the legalities of the adoption procedure, and of personal warmth or understanding at the time of childbirth and parting may have been more clearly recalled. The elapse of eight or more years (average 19) during which the long-term realities of relinquishment had been faced may have altered the perception of many mothers in this sample. The low level of satisfaction may also be related to the fact that this was a self-selected group who were mostly seeking contact with their children.

Feelings and support after relinquishment
The mothers recalled a range of feelings in the first months after they had placed their child(ren) for adoption. Viewing the past through their present circumstances, they revealed that dealing effectively with the reactions of sadness and loss had been difficult after more than half the placements.

One mother described the experience of 'searching' for her child, which has been noted in other similar studies.[10]

I looked for her everywhere in the streets of Glasgow, but I had not seen her so I did not know what she looked like.

Other reactions included a sense of unreality, confusion or denial.

It did not seem to be happening to me at all. It was somebody else.

It was as if I was in another world.

He was not really adopted but would come back to us if I could only marry the father.

50

Anger and resentment.

I was always arguing after that.

Bitterness towards my mother consumed me. She knew what having a baby meant. She was a mother herself and I couldn't understand it.

Inadequacy and frustration.

How could I cope with the nightmare of losing my baby?

I wanted to stop the secrecy, to tell the truth instead of living this lie and trying to be two different people.

Isolation and rejection.

I couldn't face anybody, so I didn't go out for weeks.

Completely alone. I coped with everything myself and went quite numb, not allowing myself any feelings.

My father died and I felt he had abandoned me because my mother totally rejected me after the baby was born.

Guilt or shame.

I was miserable because I felt I had committed an unforgivable sin which God would punish.

I felt so guilty. How could anyone give a baby away?

Fear of the future and anxiety about the child.

I was desperate to hear how my daughter was getting on.

The future held nothing for me after that.

In 39 (75 per cent) of the placements, the mothers considered that no support, whether from professionals, family or friends, had been available to them during the first 12 months after the birth. These feelings were especially likely where mothers had relinquished more than one child. In the rest (25 per cent) of the placements, mothers considered that they had had some support but in only eight (15 per cent) felt that this had been as much as they really needed. Friends of either sex or family members, including in some cases their own parents, were regarded as showing most understanding and offering greatest assistance. However, others considered that their parents were too caught up in their own feelings to be helpful or were too involved in influencing the decision to have the baby placed for adoption to be an appropriate source of comfort.

> I think you alone are the only one who can help yourself but you do need help to do this by talking things through with somebody who can be honest and objective. People at work were sympathetic and I did use them at times.

> I had one very old friend who just let me talk and cry while she sat and listened.

> The baby's father was the only one who could share my feelings.

> My new husband and his family were really marvellous. I often dissolved into uncontrollable sobbing with them.

After nearly three-quarters of the placements (38), the mothers believed they would have been able to talk to others about their feelings and gave examples of the areas they considered to be of most importance to themselves at the time. These included talking about the child and the adoption.

> I wanted to say that it was not really what I wanted to do – it was done for the sake of everyone else.

> It was like having a stone wall in front of you and no way out. I needed to justify that I had done the right thing, that it was best for me and for him.

> I wanted to say, 'Tell me about her. How is she getting on, is she happy and settled?'

Some mothers wanted to talk about their feelings about the other people involved, such as their parents or the baby's father.

> I wanted to discuss my feelings of resentment about my parents' treatment and how miserable I was because I felt men could not be trusted.

Most of all they wanted to be able to express their feelings about themselves.

> I needed to tell somebody how I felt. I was being torn apart and I felt death would have been easier. To say how bad I felt about it and

how I could never forgive myself, how hurt I was and how unwanted by anybody.

All that anger and so helpless. What could I do and who could help me?

I had to say how bad I felt about myself and how wrong it was that I should have given my baby away.

It was the emptiness I couldn't understand. I felt as if I had given my own life away.

Triseliotis and Hall[11] found a very similar sense of neglect of personal feelings to be prevalent in their study of Scottish mothers who were interviewed within a few months of parting with a child. In none of the 39 placements in this study where mothers had wanted to talk about the relinquishment was this possible 'as much as needed'. In three cases, mothers said they were able to talk to a 'considerable' degree and another to a 'moderate' degree, while this had only been 'a little' after the other 16 placements. The people they talked to were most often friends or flatmates, their child's father or another partner, or family members. Some were reduced to speaking to anyone who would listen to them, or else they clammed up after attempts which had been unsuccessful.

Where they thought they would have been unlikely to express their feelings (13 or 25 per cent), mothers were mainly inclined to the view that nobody could have helped them to recover their equilibrium or that talking would only have made things worse for them. Others recognised that they had 'bottled up' their true feelings and thought that releasing them might have been of therapeutic value but felt temperamentally unable to respond to this form of help.

In the absence of appropriate support, many of the mothers were able to recognise that they had in fact expressed their feelings in a variety of different ways, for example by returning to work as soon as possible; by entering into a new relationship; or by withdrawing completely, sometimes suffering bouts of sadness and depression which included some attempts at suicide.

I drifted further and further from my own family, rejecting them as they had done me. I lost my self-respect and this led to a lack of control, forethought and direction. Drugs, drink and promiscuity were the result. I became unable to trust adults and made myself thoroughly objectionable and argumentative. Eventually I became very depressed and tried to kill myself by taking an overdose.

I went back to work as soon as possible but I was very low for a long time. I worked hard to realise my career ambitions and to improve my material standards. I was too proud to let them see that I was upset but I became very defiant, obstinate and angry. It made me much harder. I did as I was told to do – worked hard at my chosen career and I have never talked to anyone about it until today.

My escape was to marry soon afterwards and have two children as quickly as I could but that was a mistake because I had a dreadful home life and began to drink heavily.

References

1 Marsden D *Mothers alone* Penguin 1969; Ferri E *Growing up in a one parent family* NFER, 1976; Ferri E and Robinson H *Coping alone* NFER,1976.

2 Hopkinson A *Single mothers – the first year* Scottish Council for Single Parents, 1976.

3 See 1 above, Marsden.

4 See 1 above, Ferri and Robinson.

5 Triseliotis J and Hall E 'Giving consent to adoption', *Social work today* 2 17, 1971.

6 Raynor L *Giving up a baby for adoption* ABAA, 1971.

7 See 5 above.

8 See 6 above.

9 See 5 above.

10 Pannor R, Baran A and Sororsky A 'Birth parents who relinquished babies for adoption revisited' *Family Process* 17, 1978; Millen L and Roll S 'Solomon's mothers: a special case of pathological bereavement' *Amer J Orthopsychiat* 55 3, 1985; Watson K 'Birth families: living with the adoption decision' *Public Welfare* Spring, 1986.

11 See 5 above.

6 Long-term effects of relinquishment

All the relinquishing mothers in this study were looking back to events which occurred at least eight years before. During the intervening period, many other major events had taken place in their lives. We extended the question used in the Australian study to include all of these developments rather than just those in the last 12 months. However, respondents were asked to focus especially on the most recent events.

Major life events experienced after relinquishment
The same broad categories as those identified earlier for pre-relinquishment events emerged as the most relevant:

- insecure environment (80 references)

- experiences of death or separation (35 references)

- positive experiences (49 references.)

Insecure environment
This was characterised by poor relationships with parents or partners; violence and abuse; alcoholism; ill health; financial or housing worries; problems with other children.

> I was a battered wife. My husband was an alcoholic who badly abused the children.

> We separated several times before our divorce. It was partly my fault. I was so anxious to replace the daughter I had lost that I took out my feelings on everyone.

> As a single parent I have struggled to bring up my children, coping with my daughter's alcoholism and watching her gradual degeneration. I think she has suffered because she was born so soon after I parted with the baby for adoption.

Death or loss
This was of family members, especially partners or other children, and close friends.

> My father who meant everything to me was terminally ill for a year and suffered terribly before he died. My mother said I was to blame and I really believe it although it was years after the adoption.

> My mother began to drink secretly and I couldn't confide in anyone, especially not my father. He committed suicide when he found out.

> Deaths in the family have produced pathological reactions for which I needed therapy. The problem is controlled but not resolved.

> I have lost several very close and dear friends from cancer. Every time this happens my feelings of loss seem to get worse rather than better.

> I have lost my other children following my divorce. Access is being denied to me and the fact of having had a child adopted is being used to show that I am an uncaring mother.

> I have experienced many tensions and great unhappiness due to failure to conceive. Every time an IVF treatment was unsuccessful I experienced once again the loss of the baby I had given up for adoption.

> It nearly broke my heart when my boyfriend and I broke up after many years together. I felt completely rejected.

Positive experiences
These were of happy marriages, more children and their achievements, and the mothers' personal academic or career successes.

> Five years later I married the child's father and we are very close. I believe this is partly due to our shared experience of having had to part with our only child for adoption.

> When my adoptive mother died I felt able to trace my natural mother. This has answered many questions and settled me effectively.

> When I obtained this job I became completely independent financially. It has given me monetary rewards and enhanced my

self-esteem as I am very suited to the job and have made a real success of it.

My husband and children are the best things that have happened in my life. I had to wait five years before having more children. I believed I was being punished for giving up my baby.

Stress of relinquishment compared with other major life events
After they had recounted the major events in their lives, both before and after relinquishment, the mothers were asked to compare them with the experience of placing their children for adoption. The comparison was made according to a scale which rated the severity of stress they had experienced as a result of the relinquishment. The answers given by the mothers in the no-contact group are reported separately in Table 12 but were little different from the replies of mothers in the contact group.

Table 12

Perceived degree of stress caused by relinquishment

| Relinquishment | Contact group | | No-contact group | |
	Number	Per cent	Number	Per cent
Moderately stressful	3	7	1	20
Severely stressful	15	37	1	20
Most stressful life event	23	56	3	60
Total	41	100	5	100

Interestingly, only one of the mothers who had experienced two or more relinquishments said this had been 'the most stressful thing' she had experienced. This was the mother who lost all three of her children at the same time. The others had been involved in events which they considered even more severe or else found that the immediate problems of daily life were more stressful.

Comments made by those who rated the relinquishments as 'moderately stressful' indicated that, even when other events had had a more crushing impact, these were sometimes a cumulative experience.

I have lost four more babies, through miscarriage, each more stressful than the last.

It isn't just giving up the baby that is stressful, it is having the baby in the first place. Having a miscarriage was more painful because it was also a loss and, that time, the baby was very much wanted.

My sister's illness and death were the worst, then my father's death. I have not allowed myself to feel self-pity over the adoption; perhaps that is why it seems less stressful.

Mothers who considered that the adoption placement(s) had been 'severely stressful', but not the 'most stressful' event in their lives, clearly weighed up the distinction very carefully.

The birth itself was more stressful, knowing I could not keep my baby or even see or hold her.

Giving up my baby was almost as stressful as the death of my husband and much more so than the physical injuries of my violent first marriage.

My daughter's death was more severe but at least I have five years of valuable memories. I have had to put all this to the back of my mind for so long that assessment is difficult. At least the baby was going to good parents.

The torture of possibly losing my other two children when they went into temporary care was more stressful.

A deep sense of bleakness and despair comes out in the comments made by those who rated the relinquishment experience as the 'most stressful' event in their lives. They felt that 'nothing' could be 'worse' or 'so disastrous' and were haunted by memories and heartbreak which went 'on and on' so that 'the stress continues forever'. A frequent comparison was made with death.

It is like a death but you cannot let the feelings die. They resurface at every stage.

It compares with the death of my parents but it is so much more difficult to deal with because I have never been able to talk about it.

Nothing will ever compare with it. What could be worse than losing yourself and then have to go on living?

Nothing compares with the stress surrounding the birth itself, the loss of any power, absence of choices, helplessness and finally the pain of the bereavement itself.

When we examined the factors which might be associated with these ratings for the 37 mothers in the contact group who spoke to us about relinquishing just one child, we found that they were in accord with the experiences surrounding the pregnancy, birth and adoption described in the last two chapters. The numbers were too small to test statistically for significance but the results showed that mothers more often found the relinquishment the 'most stressful' event if they:

- moved from their home community when pregnant

- went to a Mother and Baby Home

- did not feel the adoption decision was as they wanted

- considered changing their mind

- were dissatisfied with the way the adoption was handled

- had no support in the first 12 months afterwards

- did not feel able to express their feelings.

Another finding from this analysis was that nine (or 82 per cent) of the 11 mothers whose children were placed through local authority adoption agencies rated the relinquishment experience as 'the most stressful' event, compared with 50 per cent of the 26 mothers whose children were placed by voluntary agencies. The mothers had not been asked to comment on the agency organising their adoption, so this result was less predictable than some of the other associations.

A study of agency practice in the 1960s[1] found that local authorities were in a 'slightly less favourable' position than voluntary societies with regard to the use of trained caseworkers, but 'trained staff were generally scarce among both types of agencies'. The local authority workers carried higher average caseloads than the voluntary society workers and there also appeared to be various factors which influenced the referral of mothers to the different types of agency. The local authority workers were said to feel that they were 'usually left with the less rewarding cases'. This attitude could have increased the stress experienced by relinquishing mothers who were in touch with local authority agencies.

However stressful they had found the relinquishment experience, hardly any of the mothers had sought counselling to help them come to terms with it. Two of the three women who had done so, and found it helpful, were in the no-contact group. Although it would be interesting to speculate whether this indicates a link between the receipt of counselling and the lack of desire to contact their child, the numbers in the no-contact group were too small to explore this possibility. Conversely, there may be a link between the conspicuous lack of reported use of counselling at all stages in the relinquishment process within the contact group and the wish to seek a reunion. Some of the reasons mothers gave for taking this step are explored in chapter 7.

Changes in feelings since adoption

Looking back over the time since their children were adopted, some mothers in the contact group found it difficult to assess their feelings. While over half replied that these feelings had intensified and 17 per cent said they had weakened, a further 17 per cent considered that they had changed but were neither stronger nor weaker. Three mothers thought their feelings had remained unchanged. The Australian study related the question more specifically to a 'sense of loss' but also found that some relinquishing mothers considered that this had remained the same.[2]

Almost all the women considered that their feelings about the relinquished child became stronger at particular times of their lives. The main triggers to these feelings were:

- anniversaries of the adopted child's birth or adoption

- family occasions – births, weddings, gatherings, Christmas and New Year holidays

- deaths and illness, including miscarriages

- children – in general and birth mothers' own – birth, developmental progress

- media coverage on related topics – adoption, separation, bereavement.

Table 13

Changes in feelings since adoption

Feelings	Contact group		No-contact group	
	Number	Per cent	Number	Per cent
Unchanged	3	7	0	–
Intensified	23	56	4	80
Weakened	7	17	1	20
Changed	7	17	0	–
No answer	1	2	0	–
Total	41	100	5	100

They described some of these occasions in more detail.

I think of him on the date he was born every year – opening his cards and presents – it is sad.

Christmas and New Year are the worst – there is always that one missing at family gatherings.

I have nephews and nieces of similar ages and I live with these reminders.

Watching anything on TV about adoption or reunions of people who have been separated from each other, like *Surprise, Surprise*. The tears just roll down my cheeks.

Current thoughts about the child

When asked how often they now thought about their children, 85 per cent of mothers in the contact group replied that they did so every week or even daily. It was clear from the circumstances described that the children were a constant presence in many mothers' thoughts.

She is part of my life; every day I wonder how she is and whether I will ever see her again.

He remains part of the past and the present.

It is as though they were just away somewhere.

Table 14

Frequency of thought about children

Frequency	Contact group		No-contact group	
	Number	Per cent	Number	Per cent
Often (including daily)	35	85	1	20
Sometimes	6	15	3	60
Rarely (less than once a year)	0	–	1	20
Total	41	100	5	100

Those birth mothers who frequently thought about their children, often in response to a particular stimulus, and who were still feeling their loss most acutely showed much of the special kind of anxiety which was identified by Dr Colin Murray Parkes:[3] 'I think it is fair to say that the pining or yearning that constitutes separation anxiety is the characteristic of the pang of grief'; and 'pining is the subjective and emotional component of the urge to search'.

Some of the needs and activities expressed by this group of birth mothers coincide with those observed in the bereaved or in children who have been separated from their parents. This includes the sense of having 'to look for him everywhere' or continuing 'to imagine I have seen him'. Some adopted children are also known to show similar behaviour until they have again met up with their birth parents.

On the whole, mothers contained and even welcomed these thoughts, but a third said they sometimes had to stop themselves, for example, if they found they were 'starting to become depressed about it'. Then they would do things like 'paper a wall or clean out a cupboard' to try to take their minds off the subject. Others held the view that stopping thinking about the child would be 'another way of rejecting her, a betrayal to both of us' or still wanted 'to feel the pain' so as not to feel they had 'completely lost touch'.

It was more usual to accept these thoughts because the mothers believed it 'important to keep him in mind' or because 'it means I am prepared and positive if he should seek me'.

Assessment of the relinquishment experience

The mothers' comments on the negative or positive aspects of their experience of having placed their children for adoption emerged as overwhelmingly negative, but with some positive aspects.

Negative aspects

- Fears about the child – anxiety about the adoption and the child's wellbeing.

- Unhappiness arising from the experience of loss, guilt and poor self-image.

- Poor personal relationships due to family tensions and the secrecy surrounding adoption.

Positive aspects

- Birth mother's own increased maturity, independence and sensitivity to the needs of others in trouble, especially pregnant girls.

- The firmly held belief that adoption was to the advantage of the child by offering greater opportunities and escape from later traumatic events in the life of the birth mother.

Despite the predominance of negative views, their current assessment of the meaning of the relinquishment experience was clearly affected by the decision of the mothers in the contact group to take steps to register their interest in a reunion. Their replies were tinged with anticipation, as well as apprehension, about the possibility of future contact. Mothers were aware that taking this step could bring reassurance about the past but could also add new pains and anxieties.

> There is this need to sort out the issue of contact, the preoccupation with how to go about it and to seek reassurance that my strong need to know does not mean there is something wrong with me emotionally.

> I will continue to feel it was the wrong thing to do and to face the reaction of friends who think I should not or need not have given her away. I just have to hope she will include me in her life again.

Fear – that he has not had the security I thought he would get after all, and longing – for him to get in touch.

I am living in the hope of hearing from her next birthday but what if she doesn't come? There is the anxiety about the future. Will she contact us or will we never know?

Degree of adjustment achieved

Looking back over just the previous 12 months, one in four mothers felt that they had adjusted 'extremely well' to the relinquishment experience while, at the other end of the scale, one in seven did not feel they had adjusted 'at all'. Overall, 37 per cent felt they had adjusted well or extremely well; 26 per cent moderately; and 37 per cent poorly or not at all.

Table 15

Perceived degree of adjustment to relinquishment (in last 12 months)

Adjustment	Number	Per cent
Not at all	7	15
Poorly	10	22
Moderately	12	26
Well	6	13
Extremely well	11	24
Total	46	100

The range of ratings showed a good distribution, which had been a concern in the Australian study.[4] However, a somewhat higher percentage of mothers in Winkler and van Keppel's national sample than in our study rated their adjustment as good (49 per cent compared with 37 per cent). When our sample was divided into the two contact groups, three out of five mothers in the no-contact group felt they had adjusted 'extremely well', the other two 'poorly'.

'Adjustment' was regarded by many women to be a difficult word to interpret or apply to their situation. Although two out of three mothers felt they had made efforts to cope with the effects of parting with their children, about one-third felt that they would never be likely to adjust. Some still got very upset and angry or did not see how they could 'come to terms' with an experience which was 'not of my own free will. I shall always feel guilty'. Others said that 'despite the regrets and sadness', they felt they had made the right decision or were even more positive.

> I feel I have adjusted extremely well and have really no regrets about it. It was the right thing for both of us at the time.

> I feel I made a very silly mistake which would not have happened these days. I have tried not to let it affect the rest of my life but that does not mean that it was or is easy.

> I believe I have adjusted extremely well but I have had to work very hard at it and will always have to. I have never asked myself whether it was the right or wrong decision because it was the *only* decision I was able to make at the time. Being able to admit it openly, though it wasn't an easy thing to do, has helped me to cope.

Among the 37 mothers in the contact group who spoke about relinquishing one child, we found that the factors associated with good adjustment (rated by them as 'well' or 'extremely well') were more often:

- now aged under 40

- married

- had a low GHQ score

- having no full sibling children

- single at relinquishment

- relinquished first-born child

- lived with parents at the time

- moderately satisfied with hospital experience

- saw child in hospital

- placed child through a voluntary agency

- adoption decision was 'as wanted'
- did not change mind about adoption
- satisfied with the way the adoption was handled
- received support in first year
- did not want to talk about the relinquishment
- feelings since have weakened
- sometimes think about child now
- found relinquishment 'moderately stressful' compared with other major life events

Family influences and adjustment

Adjustment, or living with relinquishment, was affected by the degree of secrecy about the adoption maintained within the birth mother's family. In spite of the fact that only two mothers said they had told nobody at all about the relinquishment, many had kept this secret from at least one member of their immediate family. This was most likely to be their other children or close relatives.

In the 19 cases (41 per cent) where other children had not been told about their brother or sister, this usually affected all of them, but sometimes mothers had told some children and not others. Either of these situations could cause difficulties.

> I know I should have told them, and the fact that they have grown up without knowing is of great concern to me. I fear the possibility of their finding out from somebody else and their reaction to the situation if they were told. I have always been determined to be a good mother, an adequate provider even though I brought them up on my own, and I suppose I am fearful that the discovery of the adoption would lower me in their estimation.

> My other daughter and son do not know about their brother. This is a worry as I want to tell my daughter, who is quite old enough to understand. My husband doesn't want them to know but I think it is important for the future.

Only one woman had not told her husband of the relinquished child. Many emphasised the importance of sharing this information, usually at the outset of a close relationship, despite their fears and – not infrequently – the adverse results of their openness.

Table 16

Personal relationships affected by relinquishment

Relationships affected	Number (out of 46)	Per cent
Children and grandchildren	36	78
Parents	35	76
Husband	32	70
General	20	43
Own siblings	11	24

Almost all the mothers considered that their personal relationships had been affected by the relinquishment. Parents, partners and children were mentioned most frequently but a more general and pervasive effect was perceived by some. Over the years, some relationships had healed but others remained strained.

> It drove me further from my parents. We were never close but they felt 'let down'. They have never expressed any regrets about the adoption and there is no recognition of its effect on me.

> The underlying resentment against my parents is now under control. I have forgiven them and we are close now. I think they were as helpless as I was.

> We have a special, poignant marital relationship with angry feelings surfacing more often in the beginning but these abated when my husband's own distress and self-recrimination were apparent.

> My husband is vehemently against adoption and therefore I have not told him about my child. This is the cause of considerable tension which underlies our relationship.

> I am labelled a bad mother for the past. I believe my depression and drinking have ruined my life and relationships, especially with my children.

It has made me determined to be a friend to both my children and to try my best not to let them down. At least if things go wrong I feel we can talk about them.

I am very self-conscious, not easy to get to know. I cannot confide in people and they don't really know what I am like. It is not easy to talk to other people and I can be very easily angered or upset.

Possible effects of relinquishment on health and wellbeing

A consideration of the possibility that there might be links between the mothers' experiences of placing a child for adoption and their perceived state of current health took into account the fact that the study included women from a wide range of personal and family circumstances (see chapter 3).

For example, it was hardly surprising to find that women aged 40 and over more often reported that they suffered from poor physical health than younger women. Similarly, women who were not working more often said they were in poor health than those currently in employment. Women who had never married or whose marriage had ended also more often reported poor physical health than those who were currently married.

Further examination of variables relating to relinquishment experiences indicated few links between the mothers' perceived current state of physical health and events surrounding the actual adoption placement (such as whether they saw the child, or whether the decision was according to their wishes, or whether they were satisfied with the way the adoption was handled). However, there did seem to be more of an association between current health and subsequent feelings about the relinquishment. Mothers who said they did not receive any support during the first year after this event more often reported that they were now in poor physical health than those who were helped.

All those whose feelings about their child remained unchanged said they were now in poor health and those whose feelings had intensified considered they were more often in poor health than those whose feelings had weakened. Similarly, one in four of those who thought about their child frequently said they were in poor health compared with none of the mothers in the contact group who sometimes thought about them. Nevertheless, the proportion of mothers reported to be in poor health, and who considered they had made a good adjustment in the previous 12 months, was very similar to that of mothers with poor adjustment.

Although women who said they were in poor physical health had higher average GHQ scores than those whose health was reported to be very good, the relationship between emotional health and other factors did not always follow the same pattern. For example, there had been little difference in the current physical health of women who did or did not have other children, but the average GHQ score for those with children was 4.0 compared with 1.2 for those without other children (using the GHQ method of scoring; see chapter 3).

There was some further evidence of stresses in bringing up other children, which may possibly have been increased by the mothers' relinquishment experiences. For example, mothers who had other children who were full siblings to those placed for adoption had higher average GHQ scores than those whose children were half brothers or sisters. Also, mothers who said there were close family members, often their children, who did not know about the adopted child had slightly higher GHQ scores than mothers who were not hiding this secret.

Mothers who felt the decision to place their child had been based completely on their wishes had lower average GHQ scores than mothers who felt more negative about this decision. There was no difference in the scores of mothers who were satisfied or dissatisfied with the way the adoption was handled, or between those who wanted to talk about their feelings about the relinquishment and those who did not. Those who were given support by their family, friends, social workers and others during the first 12 months after relinquishment had average GHQ scores of 1.0 compared with 4.4 for those who did not receive this help. Similarly, those who thought about their child sometimes had lower scores than those who still frequently had them in mind.

Interestingly, mothers who said their feelings about their child had changed since the adoption had higher average scores than those whose feelings had intensified, but not as high as those whose feelings remained unchanged. Mothers whose feelings had weakened over the years had the lowest GHQ scores of all. Yet, when mothers compared the stress of relinquishment with other major events in their lives, there was almost no difference in GHQ scores between those who had found the adoption the 'most stressful' event and those who had experienced other events which were more stressful.

Earlier in this chapter it was reported that mothers who rated their adjustment in the previous year as good had lower average GHQ scores than those who rated their adjustment as poor. In fact, mothers who said they had adjusted 'well' had even lower scores than those who gave the most positive reply of 'extremely well'. This is a useful reminder that pressures quite outside the relinquishment experience may have been influencing the mothers' current state of wellbeing.

References

1   Triseliotis J *Evaluation of adoption policy and practice* University of Edinburgh, 1970.

2   Winkler R and van Keppel M *Relinquishing mothers in adoption* Melbourne Institute for Family Studies, 1984.

3   Parkes C *Bereavement: studies of grief in adult life* Tavistock Publications, 1972.

4   See 2 above.

7 Expectations of future contact

Almost all the mothers in this study were hoping at some stage to resume contact with the children they had placed for adoption. Some knew that they would have to wait at least until the children were aged 17 and old enough to initiate a search. Others, whose children were now into their late twenties or thirties, must have wondered about the chances of contact. If they had seen television programmes and other media coverage, or read any of the previous research on the subject,[1] they would have been aware that the possibility was always there, as a few adopted people leave their searches until they themselves are middle aged. By registering their interest in contact with Family Care's Birth Link service, these mothers at least had ensured that the process would be facilitated if it was a mutual wish.

Knowledge of legal rights

The law as it stands makes little allowance for open adoption in which contact can be either maintained or initiated between adopted children and their birth parents. The courts have been extremely reluctant to attach any terms or conditions, such as contact, preferring to leave any arrangements to the parties involved. Such indirect evidence that exists on the value of openness within adoption 'appears to stress the need for maximum autonomy' of the adoptive parents.[2]

All the participants in the study were asked whether they had been told at the time of the adoption that in Scotland the law allows children who have reached the age of 17 access to their original birth records and, if they wish, the right to seek out their birth parents.

Thirty-three (72 per cent) of the 46 women replied that they had not been told this when they relinquished their children. Many said they had acquired the information comparatively recently, mainly from unofficial sources. Often they had heard about the changes in England and Wales and assumed that, therefore, the law in Scotland was changed at the same time. Many of them thought 18 or 21 was the age at which access to records was allowed in Scotland.

The birth mothers were also asked whether they thought relinquishing parents should have the reciprocal right, once the child reached 17, to find out about the adopters and, if they wish, seek out the child. Changes to the law would be required to provide this right, which is already in effect in New Zealand, parts of Canada, Australia and the United States.

Table 17

Should birth mothers have the same rights as adopted people?

| Response | Contact group | | No-contact group | |
	Number	Per cent	Number	Per cent
Yes	27	66	3	60
No – status quo	6	15	2	40
Uncertain	3	7	0	–
No answer	5	12	0	–
Total	41	100	5	100

The mothers' responses suggested that some would need to give further thought to this, but at least 60 per cent in both groups were in favour of the reciprocal right being available. Many indicated the need for safeguards to protect the child or the adopters from possible dangers as 'not all birth parents are responsible people'. Some also thought the age should be higher, perhaps 21.

> It would help to open up the whole situation or discussion and allow mothers to initiate action according to their own individual needs. It should be their right too. There should be conditions to protect the child, but having no rights makes you powerless and increases the guilt you feel in taking none of the responsibility, even at a later stage.

> I think this is an excellent idea but I believe there should be safeguards for all sides. All contact should be made through a recognised agency.

This is difficult because it might be upsetting for the adoptive family. I would like to have the legal right to search but I do not want to be responsible for disrupting the adoptive parents or my son's life.

Although I blow hot and cold about contact I think it would be better for mothers to know they can take the initiative if they want to. It will give greater peace of mind in some ways.

One mother was unhappy with the idea of 'rights' on either side because of the anxiety that this created over whether the rights would be exercised. She preferred the situation to be equal on both sides 'without automatic rights'. Others thought the present situation should continue as 'it's better this way because they come if they really want to'. Whatever their views, these birth mothers clearly recognised the potential difficulties for either party in searching out the other after many years.

Enquiries about the relinquished child

When asked what they had been told about their rights to seek information relating to their adopted child, one in four mothers replied 'nothing'. The rest divided almost evenly into those who said they had been told they had 'no rights' and those who thought they had 'lost' them.

Despite their apparent lack of rights, nearly two-thirds (26) of the 41 mothers in the contact group had sought information about their relinquished children. Some had returned to their original adoption agency for assistance, others contacted their local social work department or the Adoption Counselling Centre at Family Care. However, only one mother found the information she received 'as she wanted' and many were 'not at all' satisfied.

The experience of drawing a blank on their enquiries could be very dispiriting.

The local social work department informed me that no information was available or possible. It was very depressing to feel you have no way of knowing if your child is alive or dead.

Some mothers obtained information which could have been passed on to them years earlier, at the time of the relinquishment, but felt 'at least it was something'. A mother, who had been helping a relative who was placing her child for adoption, made an interesting contrast between current practice and her own experience some 15 years earlier.

> I was amazed that she received so much information and was involved in all the decisions that were taken about her baby. My husband and I decided to make an appointment with the adoption agency and we asked for a photograph and a letter to tell us how our daughter is progressing. They looked up the files but there was nothing I didn't know already and they said they could not get in touch or find out anything. They told us there was nothing we could do except register with Birth Link. Now all we can do is wait until she is 17 in two years time and then we hope she will come and find us.

It was hardly surprising that all those in the contact group who had not already tried to obtain information about their children stated that they would like some. Three mothers in the no-contact group also said they would like to know something about their children even though they were not seeking a reunion. The other two mothers in this group were not interested and felt it was best to leave things as they were.

Table 18

Degree of satisfaction expressed with result of enquiry (contact group)

Satisfaction	Number	Per cent
Not at all satisfied	17	65
Fairly satisfied	8	31
Satisfied	1	4
Total	26	100

In the rest of this chapter we concentrate mainly on the feelings associated with information exchange, searching and meetings expressed by the mothers in the contact group. However, the contrary attitudes held by those in the no-contact group will also be noted as they were equally strongly expressed, albeit by a handful of respondents.

Attitudes to information exchange

The nature of the information sought by the mothers in the contact group fell into two major categories: that obtainable by *indirect* means and that which required a more *direct* approach. An indirect approach was regarded as an important first step by most respondents.

Indirect means included contact with an agency which would be able to:

- provide past and/or present information on the child and the adoption from existing records

- initiate and co-ordinate an exchange of information between birth mother and daughter or son.

Direct approaches included requests for:

- a recent photograph

- correspondence directly with the adoptive parents or even the son or daughter

- preparations for a meeting with, or view of, the daughter or son.

The women were almost unanimous in their belief that knowing the facts instead of dwelling on the range of possibilities would improve their ability to handle their feelings about parting with a child for adoption.

> We were told adoption was in his best interests and I would like to know if it was.

> I imagine all sorts of things and have nothing to go on. Sometimes they are all good things, other times all the bad things. It is impossible because you are not living with the truth so you cannot face it or prepare for the future.

> I would use it to build up a picture of a real child, her personality and feelings, as well as to satisfy my emotional longing to know how she has fared.

Another important aspect for some mothers was the need to be able to share the information obtained with other members of the birth family, either because it was of interest to them, or because it would be better to know in case contact was made by the relinquished son or daughter.

The possibility of being able to leave information about themselves, their family and their current circumstances for the benefit of their children if they were making a search was welcomed by the majority of mothers in the contact group. Four out of five mothers in the no-contact group also wanted to leave information which could help the child but this was sometimes to be accompanied by a note explaining why the parent did not wish to be contacted.

The two main areas of information which the birth mothers said they would like to pass on related to the adoption itself and to the current situation, particularly with a view to a possible reunion. These two purposes were often combined.

> I want him to know that I married his father and we have three more children, his full brothers and sister. That I never wanted to part with him and have thought about him continuously over the years. Then I will feel I have done everything possible for him until he contacts us.

One mother wanted to leave 'as little information as possible so that she would be more curious and therefore she would only be satisfied by a meeting'. Another said she preferred her son 'to contact me and get it direct'. The possibility that some adopted people might be more keen to find out if they had brothers and sisters and to keep in touch with that generation was contemplated as being 'all right with me' by a mother who said this 'might be easier all round'. The fact that one mother's husband did not yet know about the child's existence was obviously something she wanted to warn her son about, but she also wanted him to know that contact would be welcomed by her.

Interest in reunion with child

For the majority of mothers in the contact group, a long-felt need had been translated into action by increased media publicity on adoption. Others had been informed about Birth Link by an adoption agency or social work department. Although very keen to have a meeting, some were also 'nervous', 'anxious' or 'wary' about it or the outcome. They knew it could fulfil their most cherished hopes, but it could also bring problems for them or for the child, or it might never happen.

> I would love to meet my daughter. I don't know how I'd feel, mind, if she walked through my door tomorrow. Meeting her would just fill my life.

I am keen but also a bit wary of the outcome. I have handled so much stress in relationships that I shall be able to cope but what about him? At 20 he is still very young and vulnerable.

I am very keen on a meeting but no longer optimistic. When he turned 17 I thought 'well, any day now' but that was 14 years ago and I am sure now that he will not look for me.

The mothers' own feelings about a meeting were inevitably affected by the reaction they perceived as likely from other members of their family. While many knew that all their family were 'very interested and enthusiastic about such a meeting', about one in three expected a mixed reception or were more pessimistic. Difficulties were considered especially likely to occur where family members had not been told about the child or where they had been openly rejecting in the past. One mother referred to a situation which probably arises quite frequently when an adopted person starts to search by tracing the address on the original birth certificate. In this case, the reception would be positive but others might not be so lucky.

My mother was worried about what she would say to my daughter if she made direct contact at my old home address but she will just let me know immediately. She would love to see her granddaughter again.

Just under two-thirds of the mothers said they would prefer to use an intermediary to facilitate the contact with their relinquished children. The intermediary was usually seen as someone who would help both sides prepare for a momentous event.

I would prefer this. I do not know what I would do or say if she just came to the door. I would not like her to take my shock for displeasure.

I should think it would be the best way to prepare. There may be things he would worry about and I might have to face the fact that he was a junkie or had AIDS.

It will be like going into the unknown and it would be helpful to have somebody set the whole thing up and to provide further support if this was necessary.

A few said that the choice to use an intermediary should be left to the daughter or son, while some others were happy to manage on their own and felt able to cope with any kind of approach.

When asked directly how they would feel if their children did not appear to be looking for them or seeking information, just over a third of the mothers in the contact group said they would accept this, even though they would feel disappointed. Another third said that they would feel really hurt and upset, while the remaining third would continue to hope for a change of mind or press on regardless because they felt so desperate. Several mothers indicated that they would try to console themselves by hoping that the lack of contact meant their children were happy.

> It is something I live with all the time. It is a constant fear and a disappointment that she has not been in touch yet. If she never does I believe it will be because she is happy and does not need us. That is what I hope, anyway.

> She is 23 now and has not come looking for me so I have got a funny feeling that I am never going to meet her. I am going to go through life and go to my grave without meeting my daughter. If she waits until her parents are dead I will be dead as well. I just hold on to the feeling that she is happy with the folk who adopted her and not bothered about meeting me.

> Helpless, miserable and angry because of the system. Very frustrated and although the feelings of worthlessness would be revived if I felt I was of no importance to her, yet I would be pleased in one way because it would mean she was content.

> Only the hope that he will come keeps me going at times. I will be very unhappy but I know adopted people and none of them has any interest in finding their birth mother so I have to be realistic.

> I would be very disappointed but it is his choice. Maybe he does not need to search, perhaps he thinks 'if she could do that to me then she may not want to know me now'. Or 'my adoptive parents have been my parents so I don't need her'.

Expectations about meeting with child

It was hard for mothers to speculate in the abstract about what they would say to their children if they were to meet or what they hoped their daughter or son would say to them. The adoption would be a key topic, both the original reasons for choosing it and the son or daughter's experiences of the placement. The mothers also saw the event as an opportunity for the expression and release of feelings, even if these were negative or very pent up. In addition, the mothers expected that there would be many pieces of factual information to exchange about the respective families and what each was doing now.

After the initial meeting, the majority of mothers hoped that some form of regular contact could be maintained. However, they were very aware that this would depend on the daughter or son's wishes and some hardly dared to hope that this outcome would result.

My hope is that we can keep in touch and be friends if all goes well.

Just to see her from time to time would be enough. It could not be a close relationship unless that was what we both wanted.

If we get on well, he will be accepted and welcomed by us all. We would like him to be one of us but we know that that would be unlikely to happen.

It will be up to her. I do not want to intrude or pretend that I am taking her parents' place.

Some mothers realised that they would be likely to feel far more upset if, after one or two meetings, their children did not want any further contact than if they had never met in the first place, unless the meetings had gone badly. Only one in four said they could 'accept' this situation, compared with one in three who were prepared to accept that their child might not be searching for them at all. Nevertheless, several mothers mentioned that even if the children did not want to continue the contact 'at least I would have seen her and there would not just be a big blank about her'.

I would just have to console myself that I had seen him and that it would not work out if he didn't want to keep in touch anyway. Maybe I would be relieved if we didn't like each other.

I would just be getting hurt all over again. I would be very upset but it is all up to her, and if she doesn't want contact it would not work for me to pursue her.

My curiosity would be satisfied. I would try to understand. I would really like some kind of relationship but that may be impossible. He is my only flesh and blood and there are quite a number of issues which would arise.

Reasons for not wanting contact

All five mothers in the no-contact group said they had considered the question of contact with their children, often at great length, but only one showed some ambivalence about her decision. This mother was also the only one to say that other people had influenced her decision, but she felt it was best to leave things as they were at the moment for the sake of her family. Nevertheless, along with three other mothers, she would consider changing her mind in certain circumstances. The most likely situation would be if the son or daughter really needed to meet, but, even then, these mothers would want to weigh up the issues very carefully before agreeing.

One mother could not contemplate a meeting while her own mother was still alive as 'she would be devastated'. Others were more concerned about their husbands or other children. The mothers in the no-contact group were sensitive to their children's feelings but also felt the need to protect themselves. As one of them put it:

It would mean explanations, strong feelings and major adjustments in our relationships and our established life styles. I have had so much to cope with over my life that I do not feel able to face the problems that this would bring.

Interest in meeting adopters

Although contact was mainly viewed in terms of meetings between the birth mother and her child, we wondered whether the mothers in the contact group had any interest in meeting her child's adopters. One mother said she had met them at the hospital when she relinquished her child, four were uncertain, and three were not interested in a meeting; but the majority (33 or 80%) said they would like to meet the adoptive parents. For some, this was really just to satisfy their curiosity about 'the sort of people they are and to hear about their lives with my daughter'. Others wanted to say 'thank you for bringing him up and looking after him when I was unable to do it'. Several mothers indicated that they would want 'to make it plain that

I don't wish to disrupt their relationship with their son'. Others said they would only like to meet the adopters if the adopted daughter or son wanted this to happen. One mother's comment sums it up concisely:

> To tell them I do not want to take her from them, to bring her closer to me by sharing information and to let them get to know me for her sake.

References

1   McWhinnie A *Adopted children: how they grow up* Routledge & Kegan Paul, 1967; Triseliotis J *In search of origins* Routledge & Kegan Paul, 1973; Haimes E and Timms N *Adoption, identity and social policy* Gower, 1985.

2   Triseliotis J, 'Adoption with contact' *Adoption & Fostering* 9 4, 1985.

8 Services for relinquishing mothers

Most of the birth mothers in this study were parting with their children for adoption during the 1960s and early 1970s. At the same time, a strong movement arose which recognised the views of those who made use of Welfare Services. Publications of the period reflected an increased awareness of the consumer's perspective.[1] Influential as these later proved to be, and despite the fact that attitudes in the caring professions may have been changing, it is clear from this study that they had not yet had a major impact on the services provided to unmarried mothers as a client group at that time.

When their suggestions for improvements to services for relinquishing mothers were canvassed, many mothers prefaced their response with an observation about some of the fundamental changes which have taken place during the intervening years.

Changes in attitudes

> A more human approach is taken towards unmarried mothers. There is hardly any stigma left but I see things changing. We need to be careful not to let moral judgements come into play again.

Practical help

> Girls these days get all the things we didn't – the pill, abortion, benefits, houses, furniture, nursery places.

Adoption practice

> When my niece had her child adopted recently, she even got to choose the new parents and to meet them. I wasn't allowed so much as a photo of my baby.

> Now social workers encourage you to keep your baby instead of emphasising the benefits of adoption.

Openness and publicity

> Nowadays you get so much about adoption – people talking about their experiences. It's all out in the open – not a guilty secret.

Although there have been many changes for the better, most of the women felt strongly moved to record particular examples of help they would have liked to receive in the hope that these could be used constructively in future practice. Their suggestions have been divided into services they would have found helpful before and after the adoption placement.

Pre-placement services

Education and publicity
There was a strong feeling that the most important need was to make sure that young people are educated in all the general issues concerning personal relationships 'even when it does not directly affect them'. Only in discussions of this kind would young people be helped towards open communication and responsible action in their relationships with the opposite sex.

Typical of the large number of comments on this issue was that of the birth mother who maintained that 'contraception was never talked about, there was nobody to ask about protection because it was "not done" to have a sexual relationship in those days'. Effective publicity 'so that you know where to go if you do need help' and easy, local access to accurate information about where to find appropriate services were regarded as vital.

Opinion about abortion was sharply divided between those who wished the option had been available to them and those who felt they could never have considered this 'easy way out'. There was, though, consensus within this group of mothers that pregnancy termination should be available to any woman 'as an individual right'.

The absence of any alternatives was felt to have been the main cause of the immense pressure they themselves had experienced when their own pregnancies were confirmed. Most of the women had anticipated a censorious or at least disapproving response from their parents but few had expected the 'totally wrong emphasis on the "correct" thing to do'. Faced with the unanimous view of 'all the adults – from the GP to the adoption agency and everyone in between', they felt powerless to question or express their true feelings. Most found themselves being 'swept along on a tide of conformity which was everything in those days'.

Time
Many considered that, in the first instance, time was of major importance. There was a strong feeling that, given longer to decide, many mothers might find a way to care for their child. Much more individual discussion about 'personal feelings and confusion' was needed before there could be any certainty that adoption was really the mother's true choice for her baby.

While this may be seen as an optimistic and perhaps unrealistic view, most of these birth mothers were young and unsupported at the time of their pregnancy. So it is certainly possible that for some, particularly those whose relationship with the birth father recovered and continued, delaying the decision would have resulted in a change of mind about adoption. 'It is such an emotional time – quite the wrong atmosphere for any decision of importance to be taken.' The study also indicated that few of the mothers had any idea that a change of mind was legally possible after the consent form had been signed.

Emotional support
For any girl or young woman who is single and pregnant, the early weeks and months of the pregnancy are of major significance. Many of the relinquishing mothers in this study delayed telling their parents until they were several months pregnant, with the result that concealment immediately became the major focus for the family.

> There was nobody with my interest at heart, who would listen and not insist that I should do this or that.

Many agreed they might have been difficult to help because 'I seemed very independent and rebellious but this was because I was pretty unhappy at times'.

They formed the impression that the professionals were all taking a particular position and that few showed any 'appreciation of my needs and feelings'. Many spoke of the need to form a close relationship with somebody to whom they might talk at a personal and feeling level and who would remain with them throughout the whole period of pregnancy, childbirth and beyond 'for as long as necessary'. The need for 'somebody to be beside me instead of doing everything alone' was strongly felt at the time, and recalled with equal strength and emotion at the time of interview.

In retrospect, they understood the isolation of their situation more thoroughly. 'A safe place to go', where it was possible to talk with an individual who could be trusted and who was not identified with either the maternity hospital or the adoption, was regarded as essential.

An impartial reception and acceptance were felt by these mothers to be of major importance in helping them to cope with the sense of confusion about personal feelings and the changes in relationships, particularly with parents and the child's father. The following comments identify the emotional aspects that the mothers felt should have been addressed:

I needed more voice and the power to express my own feelings about how it felt to be having a baby I might have to give away.

Support and permission to say what I felt.

More attention to be given to the reasons for the pregnancy in the first place and what will happen afterwards.

A chance to talk, together with the father of the child, in an atmosphere of help instead of rejection.

You should have an objective view, from an outsider whom you can trust, to tell you how it will or may affect you.

You are so mixed up. You should be able to have a discussion with somebody who has already been through it all and knows how the decision, whatever it is, affects the mother herself.

Consensus emerged that there had been a general absence of opportunities to obtain recognition of personal needs or to receive 'proper advice, not just concentrated on adoption'. A 'hard look' at the realistic options and somebody to examine the nature of lasting effects were felt to be important.

Counselling
Few of the women considered that they had received proper counselling. Some recognised that a limited amount of advice and guidance had been offered but felt that these were of little value. One of

the reasons may be that the individual casework methods used by social workers at the time were based on the psychoanalytic theories of preceding decades.

These were based on the concept of 'individual or family pathology as the root of social problems'.[2] The approach left little scope for a social work intervention which would foster a high degree of self-determination. Nor was adequate time available to offer the depth and degree of support which are now seen to be essential in any counselling service. Adoption agency workers were further influenced by the traditional view that adoption was the best possible solution for most unsupported mothers and their children.[3]

These mothers expressed strong views on the effects which contemporary professional attitudes had on them as individuals. Their perception has naturally been sharpened by the long-term effects of relinquishment as well as being influenced by different expectations of the caring services.

> It is important to be given a realistic picture of adoption. It is not always the ideal solution. Adoptive couples can get divorced or ill-treat their children just like anyone else.

> Let them hear less about the benefits of adoption. The sound of the word – it is always weighted in discussion to make mothers and children seem different and labelled. It's like a slur on both characters, as if giving up a child is terribly wrong. The child also bears the burden. He feels flawed because he thinks he was not wanted.

> I did not know I would still be suffering from the loss. They told me I would soon forget and should just get on with the rest of my life.

Counselling, as distinct from social work support, has become widely accepted as a special discipline in recent years. It is this type of personal service which has been highlighted by the birth mothers in this study as being the most likely to have met their particular needs. A combination of advocate, interpreter and practical helper emerges as an important source of emotional support 'to help me face and adjust to reality and to make me feel more, not less, of a person'.

The role of the counsellor would include a close personal relationship. Acceptance and understanding were the qualities most emphasised, together with 'somebody to be with you, to be on your side and not make you feel you are doing something wrong'. At this time of crisis, more sympathy for the feelings of birth mothers was felt to be needed.

It is a time of crisis. Some special attention must be paid to any mother during pregnancy and especially when she has to consider the fact that she may not be able to keep her baby.

Consideration of the options

Of most importance was the feeling that 'adoption should be the last resort, that is why it is so important to know what the alternatives are'. Adoption was usually presented to these mothers as the only solution to their predicament, with little or no attempt made to say 'look, do you really want to do this? Because, if not, your life will not be ruined'. On the other hand, those who had few regrets about adoption felt it was equally important that mothers should 'be prepared for well-meaning people who will try to change her mind about adoption'.

A positive, practical attitude to keeping the baby was found to be absent in the majority of cases. Lack of parental support for keeping the child in the family, together with the convictions of social workers in child care at the time, were perceived as the main reasons for this.

My family made no attempt to offer help with caring for her while I worked.

My family took all the money I earned and I was unable to challenge them.

Although practical assistance was not available to the same extent as it is today, there were sources of support which had not been explored, and to which many mothers felt they should have been referred. They learned about them afterwards, when it was too late.

Somebody has to help you find the way out. You need money, a flat, a job and a nursery place.

I know others who got a pram and a cot for the baby but I never knew who to ask.

Although I had a job to go to, I couldn't find a nursery place for the baby on my own.

87

Mention was made of the possibilities of using foster care as a temporary solution. Those who had been given this opportunity felt that the extra time, between three months and a year, had helped them to make a calmer assessment of the situation. The continuing contact with the child had helped clarify their feelings, and the generally warm response from foster mothers seemed to compensate for the rejection some of the birth mothers had experienced from their families. However, it was recognised that fostering might cause problems for the baby in making attachments later on. For this reason, many mothers felt it might not offer a universal solution. As one of a range of options, offering maximum choice to individual mothers, it was considered to have an important place.

GP and hospital services
By the time they had reached the stage of admission to hospital, most of the mothers had been in touch with an adoption agency, usually as a result of referral by their family doctor. Few had been offered routine ante-natal care. A significant proportion were ignorant about the facts of childbirth itself. Many improvements in both attitudes and services were suggested.

> The GP is the first one in authority that you see and a sympathetic, understanding person is essential.

> Ante-natal classes and instruction on what to expect from childbirth should be available as close to your home area as possible.

> Opportunities to share these experiences with other single pregnant girls would be a great help.

In making the referral to a maternity ward or hospital, the family doctor, it was felt, should be able to alert staff to the possibility of adoption 'so that they can be prepared to respect the wishes of the mother'.

As the initial point of contact, doctors were also considered to be in a position to make an automatic referral to an independent counselling service. This should be available 'long beforehand to take as much time as possible to discuss feelings and choices'. Birth fathers should be included in these discussions jointly with the mother or on their own depending on individual circumstances.

With some notable exceptions, the mothers considered that nursing and medical services had failed to allow them to be 'a person in her own right and not just the mother of a baby'. Significant changes in attitude and in the system itself were felt to be necessary, mainly to provide some choice for the individual whenever this did not directly conflict with providing high standards of medical care.

> It would have been kinder to provide a separate place, away from the ward where mothers have their babies with them all the time.

However, there was also a strong body of opinion that seeing and holding the baby, if not necessarily taking care of it, would help those who were uncertain to make up their minds about what they really wanted.

> A change is needed in the present system which allows mothers the choice of whether or not to see their babies. This is unnatural because it makes the experience unreal and does not help mothers to confront the situation. It contributes to the difficulties of adjusting later on if you have not seen your baby.

Adoption agency practice

On reflection, it was recognised that many of these issues might have been resolved if the support of a trained and experienced professional had been available 'to come and talk' throughout the experience. An all-pervading sense of isolation from family and friends was encountered by the majority of the women. Adoption agency practice was considered to be in real need of improvement.

> Attention should be given to providing pleasant surroundings and suitable personalities – sensitive and tactful workers, trained in counselling and preferably married with children.

The frequent emphasis on policy among all the professionals encountered appeared to give an impression of prejudice and inflexibility.

> They all took a particular stand instead of assessing individual circumstances and providing opportunities for discussion.

> They held all the power and they did not encourage me to say how I really felt away from my parents' influence. She should have tried to

get my viewpoint even if it was difficult because I was so young, ignorant and inarticulate. I expected her to know or realise that I just didn't know how to stand up for my rights as a person.

Much more concern for the personal wellbeing of birth mothers was perceived to be necessary and, indeed, to form the basis of adoption practice. Few mothers felt their reception had been one of acceptance or even respect for their own view of their situation. On the contrary, the perceived attitude was of their unworthiness, an implied disapproval of their actions and a general disregard for their feelings.

Reassurance is needed but also a realistic reminder that the feelings of loss and guilt never disappear. They should quote examples from the experiences of other mothers who have given up a child for adoption. I don't think they really knew what happened afterwards.

Birth mothers' needs

The impression that the birth mothers' needs took second place to those of the baby was universal, reinforced by a strong sense of guilt and deep feelings of concern for the child's future wellbeing. Even without changing that important emphasis, it was agreed that more could and should be done to correct the balance, starting with the dissemination of more information.

You should be given accurate information in writing on the adoption process, your rights, the assessment procedures for adoptive parents and how they are matched with a child.

Misinformation or failure to clarify certain issues for unmarried mothers had been the cause of much persistent anxiety.

I put 'father unknown' in the records because somebody told me that if I gave his name he would have to be traced before she could be adopted. Now my daughter may think I really had no idea who her father was.

Placement policies

During the 1960s and 1970s adoption workers were responding to the work of John Bowlby on attachment and loss[4] and to the theories of

Erikson[5] on the development of 'basic trust' between a mother or carer and a young child. At that time it was widely believed that permanent attachment could only be achieved by placing an infant for adoption at the youngest possible age. Consequently, unless mothers returned to Mother and Baby Homes, their babies for adoption were usually separated from them soon after birth. This practice directly conflicted with the needs expressed by birth mothers for the time and space 'to breathe and think' if a carefully worked out decision was to be reached.

> I would have preferred long-term fostering so that I was able to keep the right to have her back when I married. Paying for foster care was very difficult and I couldn't afford it.

Participation in the selection of the adoptive family
With few exceptions, these birth mothers saw themselves as recipients of a service rather than as full participants in planning for the future of two individuals. The adoption procedure was regarded as a totally one-sided exercise with the agencies 'only after my baby, when I look back now'.

> As much or maybe more time should be spent with birth parents as is spent with adoptive parents.

> I give my child away to somebody I don't know. They can know everything about me but I am given no information about them. That cannot be right.

On the occasions when wishes were expressed and made known to the adoption agency, for example, on religion – the one aspect of an adoption placement on which the law allowed a mother to state her preference – these often appear to have gone unheeded.

> I wanted him to be with a good Catholic family but they told me they couldn't find one. Now he is different from me.

> My mother got them to change my instructions when I specifically asked for a non-Catholic home because of my own unhappy memories and experiences.

Adoptive parents
A clear picture of the new parents, their circumstances and person-alities, was regarded as essential in providing both reassurance that

adoption was the right decision and a basis for future thoughts about the child. Many mothers were simply told that their baby was going to a 'good home' and 'will never want for anything'. Several mentioned that they had been given a false picture, for example of a 'professional' family, which turned out 20 years later to be untrue. Others recalled details which gave them particular pleasure but which they wondered if they could trust.

While financial security, with all its material and educational advantages, was felt to be essential by mothers whose own circumstances lacked this, more details were needed 'to help me get an idea of how he would be brought up'. Participation in choosing an appropriate family for their baby was therefore viewed by many mothers as making a great deal of difference to their ability to come to terms with the act of relinquishment. There were others who did not feel quite so capable of being closely involved but felt that choice in this, as in so many other areas of the services provided, was important. Those for whom an actual meeting would have been too difficult to handle (because, in the words of one mother, of 'my feelings of resentment that they were taking my baby when I wasn't able to give her a home') would nevertheless have appreciated more information.

Meeting with adoptive parents
Significant numbers were in favour of a meeting with the adoptive parents on the grounds that 'it would make both sides more real to each other'.

> It would help to exchange information and to have actual memories which all of us could use in the future.

> The women need to have a good look at each other. You can tell a lot by exchanging a few words.

Instead of 'just assuming' that the adoption agency was going to provide 'perfect parents', and to provide the adoptive parents with an accurate description and account of the birth mother herself, it was felt important for personal contact to be made. Reservations that the two parties might not respond well to each other were expressed by several women but the risks were felt to be outweighed by the advantages which could be gained.

> It seems only right and natural that you should get a chance to

explain in person your reasons for choosing adoption if you are handing over your child to their care.

This urgent need by relinquishing mothers to be presented in a positive light was accompanied by feelings of suspicion that they were viewed as 'bad women' by society as a whole, by many practitioners in the caring professions, and by adoptive parents.

I needed to tell my side of the story in my own words to the parents so that they could help the child to understand.

Similar motives lay behind the view that a birth mother should be allowed to send presents to her baby 'so that he knows she cared'.

Views on preparation of adoptive parents to ensure that they are aware of the importance of these issues and to encourage an inclusive view of the birth mother were voiced with considerable emphasis. It was recognised that the attitude of adoptive parents was an important factor in achieving the best possible adjustment of adopted children to the adoptive status, to their sense of identity and roots, and to the outcome of any contact between parties in the future.

Changes are needed in the attitude of adoptive parents to birth parents. Before they adopt, they should hear from birth mothers how they feel at the time and all their lives.

Post-placement services

A continuing thread of similar needs and views ran through the suggestions made by the relinquishing mothers about particular post-placement services which they considered important. The focus in this section was determined by the ovewhelming opinion that parting with a child for adoption results in significant emotional damage to every birth mother. The degree to which these feelings of loss are effectively handled is determined by a complicated mixture of personal characteristics, positive life experiences and the quality of any emotional support which may be available.

Adoption agency practice

There were many suggestions for improvements in the way in which adoption itself was carried out. From their deep emotional conflict on their assessment of this issue, it is clear that real support for this group of birth mothers was lacking. This helps explain their firm emphasis on the need to change adoption practice since it affects all stages of the relinquishment.

As legal consent to adoption cannot be signed before a child is six weeks old, this provided a practical target date both for the agencies to place the child and for birth mothers to make their final decision. Arrangements were made for the birth mother to sign her agreement or consent to adoption at approximately the same time.

> Six weeks is not long enough to decide – six months would be the least. You are still too vulnerable. Who can make a major decision like that when you have just come through all those things – physical and emotional experiences and all in an atmosphere of anger and fear?

As previously recorded, few mothers recalled being told that the signing of the consent form did not make the adoption final. They therefore suggested that mothers should be informed that they can change their minds before the adoption order is granted by the court.

Information before the adoption is finalised
Greater attention to providing accurate information on all aspects of the legal process, and about the adoptive parents, was felt to be important, and specific requests were made.

> You need everything in writing to remind you. You are so confused and upset that even if you are told things you will probably forget them.

> It gave me such a shock when I learned they could change her name.

Many mothers felt keenly the absence of something tangible to 'help to make it real'.

> A copy of the birth certificate so that I don't have to think 'did I dream it, did I really have a bairn?'

> At the time I did not want a photo because I knew it would upset me but now I wish I had one. Agencies should just keep one in their records in case it's needed for the future.

> Something to remind you what the adoptive family was like –

details of the kind of upbringing they would give a child, not just about the material side.

Birth mothers felt that they too should provide a photograph and/or written information for the child and the adoptive parents. One mother would have found it helpful to be allowed to record what she felt in writing or on a tape recording at that time and at other times. There was a firm belief that more sharing would help everyone see all points of view and establish a good basis for children to have a clear idea of their own identity.

> Indirectly we can be helped through the new parents because, if they include us as part of the child's life history, things will be better later on.

Although the autonomy and control eventually vested in the adoptive parents was seen to be entirely appropriate once they had become the legal parents, there was a strongly held view among the birth parents that more should be required of adopters both beforehand and in the longer term.

The response to experience of loss in relinquishment
Recognition and acceptance of the nature of loss and the associated processes of grieving have taken place in the United Kingdom largely as a result of the writing of Dr Parkes.[6] In his studies of bereavement he was able not only to identify the common features of a reaction 'when a love tie is severed' but also to identify seven possible stages through which an individual may pass.

He made it clear that grief itself was 'a process and not a state . . . it is not a set of symptoms which start after a loss and then gradually fade away'. Although feelings may vary from person to person, there is a 'common pattern' and it is important to recognise that bereavement is 'not as simple a stress as it might at first sight appear to be'.

The teachings of Dr Parkes have been dictating practice in medicine and social work for over 20 years, and there is now widespread recognition in the field of adoption practice that relinquishing mothers are suffering a form of bereavement.[7] Bonds of love and attachment are known to be formed in the womb and such feelings are respected, for example, in work with parents who lose a child through miscarriage or stillbirth. Yet, although there are support groups or self-help organisations for those who have been bereaved in this and many other similar ways, no such help has emerged for mothers who part with a child for adoption.

Those mothers who had given some thought to why they felt society had neglected them and failed to recognise their need to grieve, were quite certain about the reasons for this state of affairs.

> People think birth mothers are monsters because they have given a baby away. Nobody can really understand because we are afraid to admit what has happened.

> How difficult it is to be receptive to somebody who has broken all the social rules and is asking for help!

In Parkes' research, a strong sense of guilt emerged as a feature in many of his bereaved patients. In this study too, strong feelings of guilt with associated anger were typical, as expressed by so many of the women and implied in the above quotations. Mothers who had parted with their baby at a very early age were affected by these feelings for the whole of their adult lives. The effect on their self-image, the way in which an individual 'consciously perceives himself',[8] was widely acknowledged. Many believed that their self-esteem had suffered to a degree that detrimentally affected their personal happiness and achievement. On the other hand, there were others who recognised that they had been considerably handicapped by their lack of self-worth but felt they had been successful in putting the whole experience to positive effect.

Changing the attitude of society
Resentment was expressed towards those who were perceived to have withheld support or who put pressure on birth mothers to accept their loss. It was felt that expressing greater understanding of their needs would have been helpful. The role played by the media in 'encouraging openness by education' and 'making society look at it all properly' was emphasised. Admiration was expressed for those birth mothers who had appeared on television despite their vulnerability in facing recognition, and in experiencing the pain of talking about their experiences.

> It helps others to get rid of the guilty secret and mothers can be seen as nice and normal people.

If we can talk more freely, then adopted children will perhaps be less angry about being 'given away'.

Publicity

Much more publicity for the services which do exist to help anyone affected by adoption was felt to be needed as a matter of some urgency. For example, the existence of counselling centres and Birth Link, the official Contact Register for Scotland, which some felt 'offers the only real hope for somebody like me', had been stumbled upon accidentally by the majority of participants in the study.

Why has nobody heard of it? There should be caravans and mobile displays which can visit all parts of Scotland. They are so easy to approach.

If everyone knew there were intermediary and counselling services they would feel safer; it would reassure adoptive parents.

Availability of counselling

It was generally agreed that emotional support was needed at all stages of relinquishment. This should be automatically available, in an open-ended contract, to a birth parent at any time.

Leave the door open for talks or phone calls – somebody to talk to just so that you can drop in for a chat or to let off steam.

However much a mother might think she is sure about adoption, a sense of loss has to be expected.

This service to birth mothers should be widespread and accessible, independent of medical services or adoption agencies, and should have a philosophy based firmly on the rights of all individuals, particularly women.

I was not considered a person by anyone and I think this is the most important problem you have to face.

All counsellors should be specially trained in the discipline and be aware of all the issues related to parting with a child for adoption.

At some time somebody should have said, 'are you really sure you have made the right decision for you?'

I needed help, I had so many problems, everything seemed to be going wrong and it was all my fault.

Any counselling service should have access to a well established contact register and should be skilled in undertaking exchanges of information and establishing contacts between adopted people and birth parents.

I never felt the need of anything else, but the contact register is such a good idea and I will continue to use its services.

There has to be an independent person who will approach an adopted person on behalf of the birth parent – someone with qualifications in counselling who can start the contact in the best possible way.

Opportunities for discussion with those who share the same experiences, either on an individual basis or in the form of group support, would be welcomed by a significant number of the women in this study.

We need a network like Samaritans, a helpline or something like that, which could put you in touch with someone who knows what it's like to part with a child and who really understands – anytime, anywhere.

I would prefer to talk to somebody who had gone through it themselves years before and could look back.

Use of groups

A direct question about the relevance of group support after relinquishment brought a mixed response. There was some support for the idea that sharing feelings would be valuable, especially in the month immediately following separation, 'to know you were not alone' and 'to learn to cope with the feelings you have'. Simply knowing that group meetings were available for use at any time was felt to be important by some, especially when specific issues arose.

I needed a discussion about whether or not to tell my son about his sister, and how to do it, from somebody who had already done it themselves successfully.

Post-adoption professional support
While accepting that adoptive parents 'like as little intrusion as possible', and that disruption to the child's life with the new family was to be avoided at all costs, there was general agreement that a way should be found to balance the needs and rights of all concerned. The best way of achieving recognition of the needs of birth parents was seen to be through the provision of a post-adoption service with the responsibility to seek out and organise an accurate exchange of information. The availability of appropriate professional support would be important for all three parties involved in the adoption.

> The system should include exchange of information over the years from the time the child goes to live with his new family.

> Adoptive parents should be recruited who are prepared to accept this and stress should be laid on both the adopters and birth parents on the importance of keeping in touch.

Some of the difficulties for both sets of parents were recognised, but the advantages of having accurate and up-to-date information for use by all the individuals involved in the adoption triangle were felt to outweigh the disadvantages.

> Good and bad news are equally important, though I expect I would feel dreadful if things were not going well.

> I am doubtful about the wisdom of having bad news and of having no way of doing anything about it.

> I don't think it would be a good thing to know too much or you might want to go intruding where you shouldn't.

> I have doubts that a true picture would be given to the adoption agency.

On balance, most of the mothers felt that knowing 'real facts instead of being left with fantasies' was their greatest need. They would want to know the truth about their child's life and were prepared to cope with their reactions provided support was automatically available to them.
A distinction was made between the kind of vital information which it was felt should be communicated to them as a right, and

99

the progress reports which might be deposited with the adoption agency for collection 'when I wanted it'.

Despite understanding that parental rights had been transferred to the adoptive parents when the adoption order was granted, only a few of the birth mothers in this study believed that the legislation intended information to be denied to 'the woman who carried the child inside her for nine months and then had to go through childbirth to give her life'.

Vital information.
Some mothers considered that significant life events, such as death, reception into care, breakdown of an adoptive family, or a situation where the child might need particular help, ought to be communicated immediately to birth parents.

> I believe I have the right to know if she needs me in any way.

Feelings about death were particularly strong. 'Fearing the worst' occurred throughout the childhood years, sometimes for no particular reason, at other times following an incident about a child of the same age which might have been reported by the media. Among the numerous emotions which lay behind this request were two which demonstrated the complexity of feelings involved, namely a sense of continuing responsibility for the wellbeing of a son or daughter, and a real but contradictory feeling that death itself would be easier to bear than continuing to suffer from imagined disasters.

> I could never forgive myself if anything happened to her but I would want to know and be able to share some of the grief her real parents would feel.

> To be there at the beginning and not to know the end cannot be right. Say he died when he was three or four, then all these years I have been thinking about him and it would have been unnecessary suffering.

Progress reports.
These were the most common suggestions by the birth mothers for disseminating information. It was felt that they would dispel any myths which might exist on either family side. Items of news could be deposited by adoptive parents with an agency 'over the years' without

disrupting the child whose 'happiness is paramount'. Birth mothers should participate in the process in exactly the same way.

Details could automatically be retained by the agency so that birth parents, adoptive parents and, later, the relinquished son or daughter would know it was always available 'if and when they wanted or needed it'.

Without revealing identifying details and always preserving the right to personal privacy, including that of the child, birth mothers felt it should be possible to include a range of important information in these reports. For some, 'just a message to say she is well in body and spirit', would be all the reassurance they felt necessary or appropriate. Others were specific about both the kind of information which was important to them and the periods of the child's life which were of most significance.

Although a small group of the women felt that they had needed to make 'a clean break', the majority found the first year after separation was extremely stressful. Some of this distress might have been relieved, they felt, by regular reports on the child's progress, especially if there had been medical problems in the first few days or weeks. The first birthday was frequently mentioned as a crucial anniversary accompanied by intensified feelings of loss.

Information during the first year reassures you that you have done the right thing, that is, if everything is going well.

It gave me so much pleasure to know that they had kept her name because they said it was so pretty. It made me feel they would be kind and sensitive parents. Choosing a special name was the only thing that I was able to give her.

Walking, starting to talk, all these are important stages – to know he is developing normally.

Great interest was shown in achievement at school, opportunities for 'good education, even private schooling, perhaps' being one of the main advantages seen to be offered by adoption.

I would have loved to hear from somebody, 'He's at school now and doing well'.

Perhaps the school could send a yearly report to the adoption society without the adoptive parents having to do it? It would spare their feelings although they would know it was happening.

101

However, several mothers mentioned the possibility that children 'might resent some of this information going to a stranger,' and felt their consent would be required.

Similar difficulties were foreseen in any exchange of photographs. These were viewed as potentially 'too tempting and disruptive'. For older children, letters were not ruled out.

Much emphasis was laid on the importance to birth parents of knowing when a child was told about being adopted and 'exactly what was said about why'. The feeling seemed to be that this was a birth mother's right 'to ensure that it was not a shock later'. Many had assumed that agencies checked to see that a child was told 'as early as possible' as they had been led to believe, but had subsequently had cause to doubt.

Medical histories were regarded as of major importance from childhood into later life.

> More information should be exchanged about medical issues, and a system created so that these can be notified or updated at any time over the years and related at once to either party.

This would have important implications for birth mothers themselves, and would need to start with improved arrangements for providing and recording care during the post-natal period, as 'many mothers move away from their home area or the area of the child's birth after they have parted with their baby'.

Accurate medical records were necessary for other reasons too. For example, one mother felt that her GP's records should have shown the fact that her first child had been adopted so that she was not asked later by one of the other doctors in the practice how her baby was. 'He was very kind and apologetic but it was so embarrassing for both of us.'

The birth mothers felt that there were several other important issues to record from their side. Marriage, especially to the birth father, the birth of any subsequent half or full brothers and sisters, notification of the death of a birth parent, and attitudes for or against contact, were all considered essential

Finally, the child's seventeenth birthday (when it is possible in Scotland to seek access to birth records) was seen as a critical time by these birth parents. They expressed the need to know something about their child as an adult, 'giving me an idea of the sort of person she has become' and, crucially, 'what she feels about her birth parents'. Knowledge of this kind was regarded as helpful whether or not a meeting was planned.

What are her feelings about contact?

Has she ever thought about trying to find me?

Am I basing my hopes of seeing him on nothing? I know laddies are not as keen to search.

This kind of information will only be made available to birth parents if there is widespread recognition that it is important, not only in the early stages of an adoption placement but also later on. This group of birth mothers was emphatic in their belief that their rights as individuals included receiving such information, particularly when a child reaches adulthood. With caution and safeguards, there would be little danger of disruption to any placement.

A system of information exchange
An effective method of exchanging information emerged as the most fundamental and valuable improvement to post-adoption support services suggested by the relinquishing mothers who participated in this study. Their suggestions for its form and content were surprisingly uniform.

Adoption agencies were seen as the natural holders of records for all the individuals involved in an adoption placement. Failure to retain records for children and birth parents was seen to be almost a neglect of their duty to offer support to adopted people who might wish to search when they reached adulthood.

If we had exchanged information, we would both know more about each other and this would help if it came to a meeting.

Even if he did not wish to meet me, at least the information would be available to him.

Strong preference was expressed for exchanges of information which would be made at regular intervals, but one mother felt that a retrospective picture of the son or daughter's childhood could be prepared by the child and/or the adoptive parents at the age of 17 in Scotland.

This could include major milestones throughout childhood, including the point at which a child was told he was adopted, together with his current status (working or student) and his attitude to adoption, his birth parents and to future contact.

Birth parents would be asked to prepare and deposit a similar account 'to provide information for the child about how his mother and father feel about him'.

Agencies should 'be allowed' to make contact with the adopters or birth parents to remind them to supply a report if they neglect to do so.

Arrangements for reunion

Many of the suggestions about arrangements for contact between birth parents and their adopted children repeated those made in response to questions already covered in chapter 7.

Since most of the participants in this study were relinquishing mothers who had registered a wish for meeting with their son or daughter, it was to be expected that their views would reflect some dissatisfaction with the present law which gives the right to information, and therefore the opportunity to search, only to an adopted person.

As the law stands at present, it seemed to embody the punitive attitudes often encountered by these birth mothers and recorded earlier.

It seems like the legal punishment for birth mothers who have done something sinful.

However, despite their longing for some form of contact, a sizeable group still maintained that the right to take the initiative in the situation should remain with the adopted person.

The use of an intermediary had been raised specifically in the section of the questionnaire which dealt with contact. It was referred to again by several mothers when giving their views on legal rights to search, mainly as an essential element but, at any rate, to be preferred. There were a number of women who felt that some mothers would definitely wish to search on their own even if no such support was made available to them.

Considerable thought had been given to the question of age in relation to contact or meetings. Some mothers felt that at 17, or even

18 as in England and Wales, an adopted son or daughter is far too young to cope with such a potentially difficult situation. Boys especially were considered too immature to withstand the emotional pressures of trying to manage two sets of parental relationships. By the age of 21, having acquired the extra degree of independence and accumulated life experience, young people were felt to be better equipped to deal with this and the other issues involved. Differences in environment, social and economic status, and educational level were all mentioned in this context.

Final points
Within the space of a single generation, society's view of the single pregnant woman in Britain has altered significantly. The stigma of unmarried motherhood has largely disappeared, taking with it much of the reluctance to discuss openly and in public debate those issues which are of most significance to unmarried parents and their offspring. The women's rights movement, while possibly less vociferous and militant in Scotland than elsewhere in Britain or abroad, has been an effective voice in demanding changes in legislation which recognise the rights and status of women. Heightened individual awareness, translated into group action, has brought about much improvement in the provision of services appropriate to the needs of unmarried mothers or single parents.

If there has been such a change, and 'revolution' may not be too strong a word, in every aspect of this subject, it is reasonable to ask why apparently out-of-date experiences are of any relevance to current adoption practice. In response, the following points seem worthy of consideration.

1 The period under review coincided with the time of greatest activity in the placement of infants for adoption. It follows that the experiences of relinquishment recorded in this report could be shared by the greatest number of birth mothers ever to have parted with an infant for adoption in this country.

2 Many women in the community, some of them now wives and mothers of additional children, may have similar needs to those identified by the respondents. The wellbeing of their families will be dependent on the degree of personal equilibrium they are able to achieve. Recognition and support for any long-term effects or

difficulties they may be experiencing should be an integral part of statutory post-adoption services.

3 Despite improvements in adoption practice, these are by no means universal and the position of the birth parent is easily forgotten or ignored in deference to the importance of ensuring the 'best interests' of the child.

4 Falling numbers of adoptions of infants and younger children mean that a dwindling number of professional workers will gain experience in this field. There is no room for complacency if standards of care for birth mothers are to be maintained and improved.

5 Recent implementation of legislation requires adoption agencies to provide a comprehensive service to all those affected by adoption, thereby making provision for birth parents. Emphasis on 'the child's best interests' in the Children Act 1975 and later Acts has raised questions about the severing of all ties with an adopted child's birth family throughout childhood.

6 Although little research has been undertaken to ascertain the effects of continuing contact with the birth family on children in permanent substitute homes, there is some evidence to suggest that young children are not adversely affected by the existence of suitable links of this kind. Older children with existing attachments to the birth family are believed to benefit from continuing such links into an adoptive placement.[9] While courts are still reluctant to grant an adoption order with a condition of contact, there remains con-siderable scope for establishing a post-adoption service which includes appropriate counselling and support.

7 Birth mothers who choose adoption do so for its permanence and the complete autonomy given to the adoptive parents by legislation. In this study, even those with an overpowering need to meet their sons or daughters emphasised their aversion to causing any upset to relationships within the adoptive family. They made suggestions for the exchange of information or conduct of a search which would continue to protect and safeguard these relationships.

8 In contrast to other western countries (New Zealand, Australia, Canada and the United States), social work agencies in Britain have not yet addressed many of the issues raised by birth mothers in this

and other studies,[10] or expressed by groups elsewhere.[11] Recognition of the rights of all the individuals involved, and the question of establishing a satisfactory system for the exchange of information, emerge as the most immediately significant issues.

9 Completely excluded in the past, unmarried fathers are now accorded certain legal rights and responsibilities in relation to their children. Issues of maintenance, contact and custody have received considerable attention. A father's right to be included in any discussion about his child's future, and to share responsibility for the decisions taken, have yet to be universally accepted and implemented.

References

1 Nicholson J *Mother and baby homes* Allen & Unwin, 1968; Mayer J and Timms N *The client speaks* Routledge & Kegan Paul 1970; Timms N *The receiving end* Routledge & Kegan Paul 1973.

2 Langan M 'The unitary approach: a feminist critique' in Brook E and Davis A (eds) *Women and the family in social work* Tavistock, 1985.

3 Triseliotis J *Evaluation of adoption policy and practice* University of Edinburgh, 1970.

4 Bowlby J *Maternal care and mental health* WHO, 1951

5 Erikson E *Childhood and Society* New York: Norton, 1950.

6 Parkes C *Bereavement: studies of grief in adult life* Tavistock Publications, 1972.

7 van Keppel M and Winkler R 'The effect on the mother of relinquishing a child for adoption', paper presented at the Third Australian Adoption Conference, 1982.

8 Argyle M *The psychology of interpersonal behaviour* Penguin, 1967.

9 Triseliotis J 'Adoption with contact' *Adoption & Fostering* 9 4, 1985.

10 Winkler R and van Keppel M *Relinquishing mothers in adoption* Melbourne Institute for Family Studies, 1984.

11 Shawyer J *Death by adoption* Cicada, 1979.

9 Conclusion

In this study, a small group of mothers who relinquished their children for adoption at least eight years previously have recalled their experiences at the time, and tried to assess the effect on their lives since then. Most of the mothers were hoping to resume some form of contact with their child and had registered with Birth Link. Throughout all the years since their children were adopted, the mothers who had registered had retained a very clear understanding of their sons or daughters as people with whom they still felt the deepest bond. They longed for news of how they had grown up and what had happened to them but, above all, they were concerned to know that their children had benefited, or at least not suffered, from the relinquishment decision.

When relinquishment had occurred, the mothers had been single or unsupported by a stable relationship. They were mostly very young. When interviewed for this study, they were living in a wide range of situations from secure and happy marriages with other children, good jobs and good health, to lonely, unhappy and insecure circumstances. However, it did not always follow that mothers who considered they had made a good adjustment to the adoption decision were those living in the most favourable circumstances, although this was more likely. Sometimes the knowledge that things had turned out well for them led to deeper regrets that they had been unable to share life with the relinquished child. On the other hand, several mothers who had experienced further crises and adverse conditions were relieved that their children had not had to suffer with them.

Although many of the memories recounted by these mothers make painful reading and contain clear messages for more caring practices, the picture is rarely one of unrelenting gloom and bitterness. In this report we have been careful to bring out the good things, the expressions of concern, and the support which meant so much when it was available. However, we cannot disguise the fact that counselling and social work advice and support were singularly lacking in the recall of almost all the relinquishing mothers in this study.

This lack meant that we had to abandon the attempt to test several of our original hypotheses about the relationship between counselling or support and other variables (see chapter 2). On the other hand, mothers provided many helpful indications of the kind of support that they would have liked to have received. Especially important were the need to give expression to their feelings of loss, the need to receive information at all stages in the adoption process, and the need for reassurance that they were not sinful, selfish people whose views should be disregarded. Even though young and upset at the time, they saw themselves as parents who had been faced with a desperately difficult decision, the consequences of which would stay with them and their children for the rest of their lives.

Comparison with other studies

These findings were very similar to those of Winkler and van Keppel,[1] although the methodology used in the two studies differed. The Australian study, with its much larger sample of 213, was able to carry out a mainly statistical examination of certain key variables. By contrast, the present study has concentrated on a more descriptive account of 46 mothers' recollections of relinquishment. Nevertheless, the 'implications for adoption practice' identified by Winkler and van Keppel have emerged equally strongly from our Scottish study. These were:

- The need for the provision of support and/or counselling facilities for many mothers who have relinquished children in the past.

- The need for the provision of services (support, assistance and counselling) to mothers around the time of relinquishment, where these do not already exist.

- The periodic release of non-identifying information by adoption agencies about the placement and the child's progress, as well as changes towards a more open system of adoption.

All of these suggestions are included in a much longer list recorded by Fitsell[2] following a discussion day held for relinquishing mothers at the Post Adoption Centre in London in 1988. Recent American studies have also reported similar implications for practice. For example, Watson[3] writes of the need for social workers and other professionals 'to modify attitudes of agency staff and those in the broader community about birth parents'.

He includes birth fathers 'as clients in their own right' and stresses the importance of the family as a 'critical support network'. In continuing to offer adoption as 'a very good plan for some children, for some birth parents and for some adopting families', Watson cautions us not 'to be blinded to the potential pain that it can cause' or to the responsibility to mitigate that pain. A range of services should be available, including 'the provision of information about the child placed, counselling and referral to support and search organisations'.

Changes in adoption practice

The right to choice and self-determination, accompanied by appropriate information and support including practical services, have long been basic tenets of good social work practice in adoption as in other areas. Yet there have been many changes in ways of putting them into effect since the 1960s and early 1970s when the majority of mothers in this study relinquished their children. These have been sanctioned and encouraged by legislative reforms, first in the Children Act 1975 and then by subsequent adoption and child care measures.

For example, the opening up of access to birth records in England and Wales after endorsement of the Scottish system[4] was the occasion of much public debate, and the more open atmosphere led to an increase in birth parents seeking similar opportunities. In Scotland these have been formalised since 1984 through the introduction of Birth Link, but the experiences of mothers in this study show that this is still only a partial solution. Many would like to have the right to seek information and possibly contact their child.

The need for standard procedures for providing information to the various parties involved in adoption, and their inclusion in the decision-making process, were endorsed through revised Adoption Agencies Regulations introduced in 1984. As we saw in chapter 7, one mother in our study was 'amazed' at the resulting difference between her own experience some years previously and that of a relative benefiting from the changes. However, the procedures require considerable input and commitment from social work and administrative staff, who are increasingly hard-pressed by other demands, so there is a constant danger that standards may slip back. In any case, the statutory provisions do not extend to updating information once an adoption order has been made, so that birth parents and adopted people may be faced with continuing gaps when attempting to make enquiries or to seek a reunion.

The questions of support, counselling and services such as accommodation have come to the fore through the implementation of Sections 1 and 2 of the Adoption (Scotland) Act 1978. These were deliberately left to the end of a long chain of new measures in the hope that they would be happening anyway. In some respects, they always have done so for expectant mothers as the imminent births required a certain amount of assistance. Nevertheless, the fact that few babies are now offered for adoption, and the majority of agency placements involve children who have been in care for other reasons and often have 'special needs',[5] potentially obscures the needs of apparently more straightforward cases. Yet the findings of this study reinforce the need for counselling and support for all birth parents who relinquish their children.

In recent years, there have been many developments in the field of counselling and the provision of support. On the one hand, methods of counselling and training in their use have been increasingly recognised as specialised skills. On the other hand, the use of groups as a means of support has become standard practice in many adoption agencies.[6] Both types of work are time consuming and, although there have been moves to encourage self-help groups which require less professional input, these can only succeed where members are willing and able to take on this responsibility.

Fitsell[7] refers to the wisdom of having counsellors present at least in the initial stages of such meetings in order to help the group with handling overwhelming and painful emotions. Many of the mothers interviewed for the present study were in tears at some point as they struggled with talking to another person about their memories and feelings, sometimes for the first time.

Relinquishment and reunion
One of the most difficult aspects of relinquishment to come to terms with was that the loss was like a bereavement, and yet the child was still alive. Since Parkes' classic study of the stages of bereavement,[8] there has been much greater understanding of the dynamics of this

process and its relevance to the experience of mothers parting with a child for adoption.[9] Our understanding of how it is possible to hold onto and maintain a realistic view of the living and growing child is opened up a little further through the present study.

Almost all the mothers who wanted to resume contact with their children said that they thought about them at least every week and often every day. Their comments indicated that for many of the women their child was still 'a constant presence' in that they included the child in their everyday thoughts and tried to imagine what he or she would be like or would be doing at the time, rather than 'holding onto' memories of the child they gave up. The mothers acknowledged that the absence of information sometimes made it hard not to fantasise, and they were aware that actually meeting the child might prove quite a shock on both sides.

Many parents have to adjust to a rather similar process of keeping in mind during absences, especially if contact is infrequent. The difference for these relinquishing mothers was that the separation had been more complete. It is possible that these mothers had been able to maintain a bond because they had found it easier to do this than going through the full process of grief and loss.

There is some support for this view from the findings relating to the small group of mothers who did not want to resume contact with their children. They had usually shut their children out of their minds except at times like birthdays, and usually wished to receive and exchange information in a much more distant way.

Their responses were similar to those of a bereaved person who has come to accept their loss and rebuilt a new identity separate from their child. They cared just as much as mothers in the contact group that adoption had been the right decision, but the thought of reintegrating their child into their changed lives was too painful for them. By contrast, the mothers in the contact group longed for reunion and still had a space for the child in their hearts.

It is important to note that, however much they wanted a reunion, almost all the mothers in the contact group were extremely sensitive to the wishes and needs of the adopted child and of the adoptive parents. They recognised that their child might not want to resume contact or, if they did, might prefer it on a very limited basis. Only a few really expected that the child would want to 'fit into' the birth mother's family as another member. However, the prospect of any opportunity to receive information or, better still, to meet, was something which several mothers said 'kept them going'. Some knew that the chances were extremely slim, but they preferred to 'stretch out a hand into the unknown' than to cling to the disappointments of the past.

The balance between loss and hope is a difficult one for all human beings to maintain. In most cases the pendulum swings back and forth and acceptance is precarious.

Where a person has died, there is finality. In adoption, there is the knowledge that the adopted child is almost certainly still alive, and it may be impossible to hold the two opposing forces in balance. While many relinquishing mothers are somehow able to reconcile the loss in a way more akin to bereavement, there are others who continue to feel a strong and living bond which leads them to hope that reunion will become possible.

Conclusion

Although current practice in adoption is shifting towards greater openness at the placement stage and the possibility of continuing contact later on, the reality is still that the separation is likely to be permanent. Helping birth mothers to part with their children and cope with conflicting and distressing emotions is a skilled and demanding task. This does not depend solely on social workers for, as the study has shown, the part played by families, partners and friends is also a crucial element in the process of acceptance and adjustment, particularly during the early months following relinquishment.

One of the obstacles to family support, particularly from parents, has weakened since the 1960s. This is the sense of stigma and shame attached to unmarried pregnancy. Nevertheless, the practical difficulties of bringing up a child as a single parent have changed very little. Thus there will continue to be situations where women feel constrained to part with their children, and the family dynamics may still have an influence on this decision.

There were examples in the study of mothers who could not bear for their children to have the same poor upbringing they had received. The unexpected breakup of partnerships, or the realisation that they were unready for the responsibilities of parenthood, or that trying to keep a second child would deprive both of them, are also likely to account for some decisions to relinquish children. There will also continue to be times when parents try to bring up their children but find this difficult, and eventually the children may be placed for adoption, perhaps against their wishes. However, there has been increasing pressure from the public as well as from professionals to maintain family units wherever possible. This is in line with the emphasis on community care for other groups in the population.

The many changes and improvements which have been taking place in adoption practice can never succeed in removing all the pain of an inherently difficult decision for birth mothers. However, those interviewed for this study have given some clear illustrations of the long-term effects of negative and unhelpful experiences which could have been avoided.

References

1   Winkler R and van Keppel M *Relinquishing mothers in adoption* Melbourne Institute for Family Studies, 1984.

2   Fitsell A 'Relinquishing mothers share experiences' *Adoption & Fostering* 13 4, 1989.

3   Watson K 'Birth families: living with the adoption decision' *Public Welfare* Spring 1986.

4   Triseliotis J *In search of origins* Routledge & Kegan Paul 1973.

5   Hill M, Lambert L and Triseliotis J *Achieving adoption with love and money* National Children's Bureau, 1989.

6   Triseliotis J (ed) *Groupwork in adoption and foster care* Batsford/BAAF, 1988.

7   See 2 above.

8   Parkes C *Bereavement: studies of grief in adult life* Tavistock Publications, 1972.

9   van Keppel M and Winkler R 'The effect on the mother of relinquishing a child for adoption', paper presented at the Third Australian Adoption Conference, 1982; Millen L and Roll S 'Solomon's mothers: a special case of pathological bereavement' *Amer J Orthopsychiat* 55(3), 1985.

APPENDIX

QUESTIONNAIRE

Number _____

STRICTLY CONFIDENTIAL   Birth Link Registration   Yes ☐   No ☐

SECTION A

We shall appreciate a few personal details to provide us with information about the people who agree to help us. All the information given will be treated with absolute confidence.

1. What is your age?

2. What is your present marital status?

    (1) Single

    (2) Separated

    (3) Widowed   ☐

    (4) Divorced

    (5) Married

    (6) Other (specify) _____

    (7) Details of any previous marriages _____

3. Current address (nearest home town only): _____

    Phone No (if any) _____

4. (a) Are you employed at present?   Yes ☐   No ☐

    (b) If Yes to 4(a), what is your occupation? _____

    (c) If not employed at present, what was your last occupation? _____

SECTION B
In this section we should like to ask you some questions about the baby you placed for adoption and your experiences at the time.

1. When was your baby born? Month _____ Year _____

                                     Sex: M ☐   F ☐

2. When did you place your baby for adoption? Month _____ Year _____

3. Was the child you placed for adoption your

    (1) First born

    (2) Second born ☐

    (3) Third born

    (4) Other (specify) _____

4. (a) Do you have any other children?   Yes ☐   No ☐

        If you answered Yes to 4(a) please give the number of Boys ☐ Girls ☐

    (b) Are any of these full brothers or sisters of the adopted child? Yes ☐ No ☐

        If you answered yes to 4(b) please give the number of   Full brothers ☐

                                                        Full sisters ☐

5. (a) At the time you placed the child for adoption were you:

    (1) Single

    (2) Married

    (3) In a stable relationship ☐

    (4) Separated

    (5) Divorced

    (6) Widowed

    (b) Did you marry the child's father after the adoption?   Yes ☐   No ☐

6. (a) At the time of the child's birth were you

    (1) Living with your parents

    (2) Living independently

    (3) Living with other relatives

    (4) Living with the child's father

    (5) Living in a Mother and Baby Home

    (6) Other (please specify) _____

(b) Did you move away from your home town or community during this time?

Yes ☐   No ☐

(c) If you answered Yes to 6(b) above please describe your feelings about this experience:

_____

_____

_____

7. (1) Did you receive any counselling before you placed your child for adoption? eg from a Social Worker:

    (a) In hospital   Yes ☐   No ☐

    (b) Adoption or other Agency   Yes ☐   No ☐

(2) If yes to 7(1) to what degree was this counselling helpful to you in your decision to place your child for adoption?

1	2	3	4	5
Not at all helpful	A little	moderate	considerable	extremely helpful

☐

8. (1) Did you receive any counselling soon after you placed your child for adoption?

Yes ☐   No ☐

If Yes, by whom _____

If Yes, to what degree was this counselling helpful to you?

1	2	3	4	5
Not at all helpful	A little	moderate	considerable	extremely helpful

☐

9. What other assistance was available at the time?

10. Who organised your adoption?

(1) doctor

(2) hospital

(3) lawyer

(4) private adoption agency

(5) local authority Children's or Social Work Department

(6) other (specify) _____

☐

11. (1) Did you sign the consent forms for the adoption?   Yes ☐   No ☐

(2) (i) If Yes, did you consider changing your mind after you gave consent?

Yes ☐   No ☐

(ii) If Yes to 2(i), how long after? _____

(iii) If Yes to 2(i) why did you consider changing your mind?

_____

_____

(iv) If Yes to 2(i) with whom did you discuss this? _____

If you did not relinquish your child soon after birth, please disregard questions 13 to 17.

12. Please rate the degree to which you were satisfied with your experiences in hospital.

1	2	3	4	5
Not at all satisfied	A little	moderate	considerable	completely satisfied

Please give details of what you found to be satisfactory or unsatisfactory

_____

_____

13. (i)   Did you see your baby? In hospital?   Yes ☐   No ☐

(ii) If Yes to 13(i), how often? _____

(iii) If Yes to 13(i), did you hold your baby?   Yes ☐   No ☐

(iii) If Yes to 13(i), did you feed your baby?   Yes ☐   No ☐

14. (i)   Did you name your baby?   Yes ☐   No ☐

(ii) If Yes, was your baby registered in your surname   ☐

or

the child's father's surname   ☐

15. Looking back, do you have any regrets about this aspect of the adoption?

Comments: _____

_____

_____

_____

16. How did your family and friends react to your pregnancy?

_____

_____

_____

_____

_____

17. (1) What were your reason(s) for placing your child for adoption? Please tick each statement which is true for you.

I was too young ☐

I was too old ☐

My physical health ☐

My emotional health ☐

My finances ☐

I was single ☐

The wishes of my mother ☐

The wishes of my father ☐

The wishes of the child's father ☐

Other (specify) _____

Comments: _____

_____

_____

_____

(2) Please rate the degree to which you feel that the decision to place the child for adoption was based on your wishes:

1	2	3	4	5
Not at all as I wanted it	A little	moderately	considerably	completely as I wanted it

☐

What were your feelings at the time you made the decision about the adoption?

_____

_____

_____

120

18. (i) Were you satisfied with the way in which the adoption itself was handled?

Yes ☐   No ☐

(ii) Was there anything which you found particularly helpful?

Please specify _____

_____

_____

(iii) Was there any particular help or support you would have liked but did not receive?

Please specify _____

_____

_____

SECTION C

1. We should like you to think back to the first months after you placed your child for adoption. Please describe your feelings during this period:

_____

_____

_____

2. Regardless of whether or not you felt you needed it, do you believe that support was available to you, from family, friends, social worker etc, during the 12 months immediately after the placing of your child for adoption?

Yes ☐   No ☐

If Yes, was this as much as you felt you needed?

Yes ☐   No ☐

Comments: _____

_____

_____

3. After placing your child for adoption did you want to talk and express your feelings about relinquishing your child?

Yes ☐   No ☐   Don't know ☐

(a) (i)   If Yes, what did you want to say

_____

_____

_____

    (ii) If Yes, to what degree were you *able* to talk and express your feelings, in the presence of other people.

1	2	3	4	5
Not at all	A little	moderate	considerable	As much as I needed

    (iii) If Yes, who did you talk to?

_____

_____

(b) If No, to 3 above, did you express your feelings in any other ways? What were these?

_____

_____

_____

4.   On the whole, as the time since the adoption progressed, did these feelings

intensify? ☐   weaken? ☐   disappear? ☐

5.   Have there been particular times or periods in your life since the adoption when the feelings you described earlier have become stronger?

Yes ☐   No ☐

Please give details:

_____

_____

_____

6. (i) Who have you told about the child you relinquished for adoption?

Please specify _____

_____

_____

(ii) Is there anyone in your immediate family who does not know about this child?

Yes ☐ No ☐

If Yes, please specify _____

_____

_____

SECTION D

1. What major events in your life would you single out before you became pregnant with this child?

_____

_____

_____

_____

2. Between relinquishing the child and now what major events in your life would you single out? (Focus especially on the last 12 months)

_____

_____

_____

_____

_____

2(a) Did you receive help or advice with any personal difficulties before your pregnancy with the adopted child?

_____

_____

_____

3. Compared with other major life events that you may have experienced please rate the severity of stress you have experienced as a result of having placed your child for adoption?

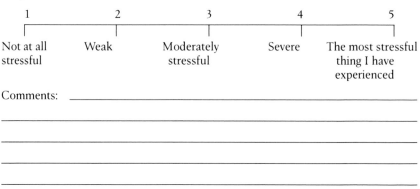

1	2	3	4	5
Not at all stressful	Weak	Moderately stressful	Severe	The most stressful thing I have experienced

Comments: _____

_____

_____

_____

_____

SECTION E

We would like to know about your *current* state of health

1. Please rate what you consider to be your current state of physical health

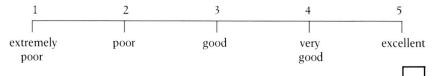

1	2	3	4	5
extremely poor	poor	good	very good	excellent

2. During the *last six months,* how many times have you visited a doctor (for personal complaints only)?

3. We would now like to know more about your emotional health, over the past few weeks. Please answer all of the questions below simply by ticking the answer which you think most nearly applies to you. Remember we want to know about your present or recent complaints, not those you had in the past.

	Better than usual	About the same as usual	Less well than usual	Much less well than usual
1. Been able to concentrate on whatever you're doing?				
2. Been feeling, on the whole, you were doing things well?				

	Not at all	No more than usual	Rather more than usual	Much more than usual
3. Lost much sleep over worry?				
4. Been feeling unhappy or depressed?				
5. Been losing confidence in yourself?				
6. Been thinking of yourself as a worthless person?				
7. Been taking things hard?				
8. Found everything getting on top of you?				
9. Been feeling nervous and strung up all the time?				
10. Found at times you couldn't do anything because your nerves were bad?				
11. Felt constantly under strain?				
12. Felt that you couldn't overcome your difficulties?				
*13. Felt that you are playing a useful part in things?				
*14. Felt capable of making decisions about things?				
*15. Been able to enjoy your normal day-to-day activities?				

	More so than usual	Same as usual	Less so than usual	Much less than usual
16. Been able to face up to your problems?				
17. Been feeling reasonably happy, all things considered?				
18. Been managing to keep yourself busy and occupied?				
19. Been getting out of the house as much as usual?				
20. Been satisfied with the way you've carried out your tasks?				

Please Note
This 20-item version of the GHQ was copied from the questionnaire used by Winkler and van Keppel in Australia. During analysis it was noticed that items 13, 14 and 15 should have been prefixed by the headings used for items 16-20. Advice was sought from Margaret van Keppel, who confirmed that the scoring for items 13-15 had been reversed to take account of this error. She also reported that the placement of the headings had been corrected in subsequent use of the GHQ. Anyone intending to use this questionnaire should do the same.

SECTION F

1. (i) What were you told about your rights to seek information about your adopted child?

_____

_____

(ii) Have you ever sought information about your child and his/her placement?

Yes ☐   No ☐

Details of information sought _____

_____

_____

126

(iii) If Yes to 1(i) to what degree were you satisfied with the information you received?

1	2	3	4	5
Not at all	fair	moderately	as I wanted	more than I wanted

☐

Comments: (eg on how helpful this was)

_____

_____

_____

2. If answer to 1(i) was 'No', would you like to know something about your child?

Yes ☐   No ☐   not sure ☐

3. How often do you think about your child?

(a) often (daily/weekly)

(b) about once every few months

(c) couple of times a year   ☐

(d) once a year

(e) rarely

(f) never

Please give details of the circumstances: _____

_____

_____

4. Do you ever have to stop yourself from thinking about your child?

Yes ☐   No ☐

How do you do this? _____

_____

_____

5. (i) Have you ever sought counselling to help you to come to terms with having relinquished your child?

Yes ☐   No ☐

(ii) If Yes to 5(i), was this counselling helpful?

Yes ☐   No ☐

6. What have been, if any, the negative aspects of your experience of having placed your child for adoption?

_____

_____

_____

_____

7. What have been, if any, the positive aspects of your experience of having placed your child for adoption?

_____

_____

_____

_____

8. What does your experience of having placed your child for adoption mean to you now?

_____

_____

_____

_____

9. We'd like you to think only of the last 12 months.

Please indicate the degree to which you feel that you have adjusted to the experience of relinquishing a child for adoption?

1	2	3	4	5
Not at all	poorly	moderately	well	extremely well

☐

Comments: _____

_____

_____

_____

_____

10. How, if at all, has relinquishing your child affected your personal relationships? Please describe any special features, eg with partner, other children.

_____

_____

_____

_____

_____

_____

_____

_____

_____

_____

_____

_____

_____

_____

11. (i) If there was a group or organisation concerned with relinquishing mothers, would you make use of it?

Yes ☐   No ☐   don't know ☐

Comments: _____

_____

(ii) Would you have used such a group at the time of the adoption?

Yes ☐   No ☐   don't know ☐

(iii) If you answered No to 11(ii), would you have joined one later, and if so, when?

_____

_____

12. (i) Are you an adopted person?   Yes ☐   No ☐

    (ii) Are you an adoptive parent?   Yes ☐   No ☐

If your answer to either 12(i) or (ii) is Yes, your comments/thoughts about your experiences with these aspects of adoption (and possibly how they relate to your having relinquished a child) are welcome:

_____

_____

_____

_____

_____

_____

_____

SECTION G

1. What are your suggestions for improvements to the services provided by adoption agencies to relinquishing mothers prior to relinquishing a child?

_____

_____

_____

_____

_____

_____

_____

2. What are your suggestions for improvements to the services provided to relinquishing mothers by adoption agencies after a child is relinquished?

_____

_____

_____

_____

_____

_____

We are most grateful for your co-operation

N.B. This questionnaire was adapted from an original used by Winkler and van Keppel.

SUPPLEMENT A

For mothers seeking a contact through Birth Link

1. What is your particular interest in contacting the Scottish Birth Link Register about the child you gave up for adoption?

    Interested only in information
    ☐

    Interested in a meeting
    ☐

    Interested in leaving information for the adopted child
    ☐

For those interested only in an exchange of information:

2. What kind of information would you like?

3. Why?

4. What gave rise to this interest?

5. What would you do with this information?

6. At any time did you find out anything about your child?   YES/NO

    If YES: What?

7. Would you like to leave any information for your child?

8. What would you wish to record?

9. Why do you feel it is important for you to leave this information?

For those interested in a meeting:

10. How did your interest for a meeting arise?

11. How keen are you about such a meeting?

12. How would you describe the urge that is driving you towards such a meeting?

    What are your feelings about using an intermediary?

13. What do you expect from the meeting?

132

14. What will you say to your child?

15. What do you hope he/she will say to you?

16. What do you hope will happen after such a meeting?

17. How keen are other members of your family for such a meeting? Who are they?

18. Have you had any information about your child since placement?   YES/NO If YES: What kind of information?

19. How keen are you to set out on a search on your own?

20. Do you have any interest in meeting your child's adoptive parents?   YES/NO If YES: Why and with what purpose in mind?

21. How would you feel if after one or two meetings you would like further contacts but your child did not?

22. How will you feel if your child does not appear to be looking for you or seeking information?

23. In Scotland the law allows an adopted child over the age of 17 to find out from Register House who his original parents were, and if he wishes to seek them out. Were you told about this at the time your child was placed for adoption?

    Yes ☐   No ☐

    How far do you think natural parents who give up a child should also have the right to find out who the adopters are, when the child reaches the age of 17 and, if they wish, seek the child out?

24. If you had this information would you search for your child?   YES/NO If YES: How?

    If NO: Why not?

SUPPLEMENT B

(For those unsure about or not interested in contact with their son or daughter)

1. Have you ever considered the question of contact?

2. How firm are you that you do not wish any contact?

3. What has made you decide against having contact?

4. Has any person influenced your decision?   YES/NO
   If YES: Who?

5. Are there circumstances which would make you change your mind?   YES/NO
   If YES: What might these be?

6. Would you change your mind if you were told that your child was seeking you out?
                                                                     YES/NO
   Please give the reasons for your answer.

7. At any time did you find out anything about your child?   YES/NO
   If YES: What?

8. Would you be interested in obtaining information about your son or daughter?
                                                                     YES/NO
   If NO: Please say why not

   If YES: What information would you like?

9. Would you like to leave any information for your child?   YES/NO
   If YES:
   (i) What would you wish to record?

   (ii) Why do you feel it is important for you to leave this information?

10. In Scotland the law provides that adopted children, on reaching the age of 17, can find
    out from Register House who their original parents are and, if he wishes, seek them
    out.

    Were you told about this at the time your child was placed for adoption?

    Yes ☐   No ☐

Do you think this is right?

Yes ☐   No ☐

Please give the reasons for your answer.

11. Do you think that parents who relinquish a child for adoption should have similar rights to find out about who adopted their son or daughter, when the latter is 17 and, if they wish, seek the child out?

Yes ☐   No ☐

Please give the reasons for your answer.

Your co-operation is greatly appreciated and your replies will be kept strictly confidential and anonymous.

British Agencies for Adoption & Fostering

British Agencies for Adoption & Fostering (BAAF) is a registered charity and professional association for all those working in the child care field. BAAF's work includes:

providing training and consultation services to social workers and other professionals to help them improve the quality of medical, legal and social work services to children and families;

giving evidence to government committees on subjects concerning children and families;

responding to consultative documents on changes in legislation and regulations affecting children in or at risk of coming into care;

publishing a wide range of books, training packs, and leaflets as well as a quarterly journal on adoption, fostering and child care issues;

giving advice and information to members of the public on aspects of adoption, fostering and child care issues;

and helping to find new families for children through the BAAF Exchange Service, 'Be My Parent'; and 'Find a Family'.

More information about BAAF (including membership subscription details) can be obtained from BAAF, 11 Southwark Street, London SE1 1RQ.